The Colic Chronicles

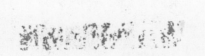

The Colic Chronicles

*A Mother's Survival Guide to Calming Your Baby
While Keeping Your Cool*

Tara Kompare
with a foreword by Shoshana Bennett, Ph.D.

Da Capo
LIFE
LONG

A MEMBER OF THE
PERSEUS BOOKS GROUP

Designed by Anita Koury
Set in 10.6 point Prensa by the Perseus Books Group

Library of Congress Cataloging-in-Publication Data

Kompare, Tara.
   The colic chronicles : a mother's survival guide to calming your
   baby while keeping your cool / Tara Kompare ; with a foreword by
   Shoshana Bennett.
       p. cm.
ISBN 978-0-7382-1169-5
1. Colic—Prevention. 2. Crying in infants. 3. Newborn infants—Care. I.
Title.
RJ267.K66 2008
618.92'09755—dc22

                        2008010015

First Da Capo Press edition 2008

Published by Da Capo Press
A Member of the Perseus Books Group
www.dacapopress.com

Da Capo Press books are available at special discounts for bulk pur-
chases in the United States by corporations, institutions, and other
organizations. For more information, please contact the Special Markets
Department at the Perseus Books Group, 2300 Chestnut Street, Suite
200, Philadelphia, PA 19103, or call (800) 810-4145, extension 5000, or
e-mail special.markets@perseusbooks.com.

Note: The information in this book is true and complete to the best of our knowledge. This book is intended only as an informative guide for those wishing to know more about health issues. In no way is this book intended to replace, countermand, or conflict with the advice given to you by your own physician. The ultimate decision concerning care should be made between you and your doctor. We strongly recommend you follow his or her advice. Information in this book is general and is offered with no guarantees on the part of the authors of Da Capo Press. The author and publisher disclaim all liability in connection with the use of this book.

Excerpts from *Postpartum Depression for Dummies* © 2007 by Shoshana
S. Bennett, Ph.D., reprinted with permission of John Wiley
& Sons, Inc. Excerpts from the Humane Society's web site were used
with permission.

1 2 3 4 5 6 7 8 9

This book is dedicated to my two amazing little girls, Leah and Lainey, my very funny and supportive husband, Mike, and my dog, Princess, who is now in doggie heaven . . .

Contents

SECTION FOUR
The Others—How to Handle Everyone Else

SECTION FIVE
*In Case of Emergency—Where to Turn When
You're on the Edge*

Foreword

WHILE ANTICIPATING OUR NEW BABY'S ARRIVAL, I THOUGHT that life would be the same as usual—plus baby—and that was that. I expected that our child would sit or sleep quietly while my husband and I discussed our day. I pictured our new baby fitting easily into our calm and established schedule and adapting to our routine. If someone had warned me that during the first few months postpartum I would be jogging the perimeter of my living room—baby in the front pack—while I attempted to eat my dinner, I would have laughed at the ridiculous suggestion.

However, that was my reality. With each lap around the room, I would grab a bite of food off my plate, gulp it down as fast as possible, counting the minutes until my husband came home and could take over. I learned quickly that if I dared stop and catch my breath, blood curdling screeches and pitiful wails would emerge from my baby's mouth. I felt that each cry was a personal criticism against me. With every cry, I heard my baby say, "How could you?

What nerve! What kind of mother are you?"

To help my baby nap during the day, I would take her out for a drive . . . may I mention that I dreaded red lights? Or, I would place my baby in her carrier on top of the running dryer. She needed the warmth and constant motion—the bumpier the better. I would do just about anything to get her to sleep and help avoid the "arched back, red-in-the face" look we were all accustomed to seeing.

Having an infant with high needs makes the already taxing job of parenting much tougher. Those ruthless, punishing lies about motherhood, including, "Good mothers have babies who don't cry" and "Good mothers know how to soothe their baby," can beat down the best of us if we're not careful.

Postpartum depression and anxiety is caused primarily by biochemistry, and it can occur regardless of how much our babies cry. However, having a baby with colic can make depression and anxiety much worse. I have worked with thousands of mothers whose main psychosocial factors contributing to their depression were burnout, depletion of energy, and feelings of failure while caring for a high-needs infant.

Thank goodness for *The Colic Chronicles*. Finally, we have a resource that directly focuses on this serious and frequent stressor. *The Colic Chronicles* dives into the raw feelings of caring for a baby with colic, and does so with a skillful blend of honesty, sensitivity, wisdom, and levity. Although *The Colic Chronicles* wasn't written in time to help me as a new mother, you and those you love, thankfully, can take full advantage. Enjoy!

Shoshana Bennett, Ph.D.
Author, Postpartum Depression For Dummies

Acknowledgments

I WOULD LIKE TO PROVIDE A VERY WARM THANK YOU TO THE following individuals:

To my girls and my husband, for allowing me the time necessary to compose this book.

To Ms. Angela Lehman-Rios, editor of *Richmond Parents Monthly*, for helping me become a published writer. It was in her magazine where my children's health column, "The Medicine Mom," first appeared.

To my agent, Ms. Lauren Galit, who played an instrumental role in landing a wonderful contract with such a reputable publisher. She was with me every step of the way.

To my very enthusiastic editor, Wendy Holt Francis, and to all of the wonderful people at Da Capo Press, thank you for helping me create my third child.

To Ms. Jodi Brown, of the National Center for Shaken Baby Syndrome, for providing me with some important resources for parents and for doing her part to help protect the lives of our children.

To Mr. George Lithco, founder of The SKIPPER Initiative, for not only sharing some important insight into the world of Shaken Baby Syndrome prevention but also for his work as a devout children's advocate.

To Dr. Shoshana Bennett, Ph.D., author of *Postpartum Depression for Dummies*, for graciously offering her expertise in the postpartum depression arena and for taking the time to help me better understand the impacts PPD has on families.

To Suzanne P. Reese, author of *Baby Massage*, for enlightening me on the benefits that baby massage offers both mother and child. She is an amazing humanitarian and champion for children's rights, and I wish her the best.

To Nancy Peterson of the Humane Society of the United States, for her invaluable information regarding the best ways to prepare your dog for a new baby, and also for her personal advice concerning my dog, Princess.

Introduction

YOU FEEL AS IF YOU'RE ABOUT TO LOSE CONTROL. YOUR BABY won't stop crying and you're tired, hungry, and all alone—not to mention you probably can't remember the last time you took a shower, but that's the least of your worries. What matters most is figuring out how to get your baby to stop screaming her head off! You've tried everything, but nothing works. Hunger, soiled diapers, and teething have all been ruled out. You've read all the right books, watched the best videos, and enrolled in parenting classes—yet all of your attempts at soothing your baby have failed, miserably. When you look in the mirror, all you see is a failed mother.

Sound familiar? I am a colic survivor, and if you can relate to any of the above, then you may very well also be dealing with a colicky baby. My mission is to help you learn how to care for *yourself* so that you, in turn, are better able to care for your fussy, difficult-to-soothe baby.

This book is for any new mother who is struggling to

take a shower in peace, who is forgetful in every sense of the word, and who is constantly yearning for a few more hours of sleep. You will learn about my life with Lainey, my colicky infant, and you'll also learn from my mistakes (such as why it's important never to broil anything unless you're ready for a five-alarm fire!).

For those of you who aren't sure whether or not your baby has colic or if there is, in fact, an underlying medical cause for your infant's cries, it's best to seek a doctor's expert opinion. Although most often the cause of inconsolable crying in newborns is due to colic, your doctor can first rule out certain health conditions, such as reflux or infection, that might be the source of your baby's fussiness.

So, what's the definition of colic? Colic is most often defined using the rule of three's: crying for more than three hours a day, more than three days a week, and for longer than three weeks, coming from an otherwise healthy and well-fed infant. A colicky baby's symptoms include high-pitched screams, a flushed face, clenched fists—and bewildered mothers. Alas, there's no known cause or cure (I wish I could tell you otherwise!).

This same baby will appear to be a complete angel at birth, yet, the minute all of your friends and family leave, she will transform into a force to be reckoned with. That's because colic doesn't appear until your baby approaches the two-week-old mark. You'll undoubtedly be scared silly when you hear those first colicky wails; unfortunately, hiding under the sheets won't make the crying fits disappear. Only time, typically three long months of it, offers relief.

My hope is that this book will comfort you, inform you,

and make you laugh when you need it the most. True, I didn't think colic was a very funny experience while I was living it, to say the least. But, I did realize that sometimes it was critical to make light of my very dark situation. I'm here to tell you that like other mothers and myself, you, too, can—and will be—a colic survivor. Just have faith in yourself, and make sure to take care of *your needs* as well as your baby's. I promise, if you incorporate laughter into your colic-crazed days, even the manic type of days, your life as you know it will soon become a whole lot better.

SECTION ONE
Head Games
How to Cope with the News

The most twisted and irrational thoughts can be found spinning inside the head of a mom of a colicky baby. At first you'll try to deny your beautiful baby has colic, and then you'll likely suffer from temporary bouts of insanity. After these crazy moments pass, it's important to search for support from friends and relatives, even some of whom you may not particularly like! If you're anything like I was, you will also, at some point, feel as if the whole world is against you: the little old lady in the grocery store, the young kid driving next to you in his red convertible, your neighbor's cat. . . . You'll be convinced that they all hate you and that they have absolutely no idea what you're going through. But don't despair, you will learn to accept the current hell you are living in and do your best to survive, one baby step at a time.

1

Somebody Pinch Me

GIVING BIRTH TO ANOTHER HUMAN BEING IS ONE OF THE most miraculous and torturous events a woman can experience. After surviving months of nausea, back pain, and kicks in the ribs, you then have the pleasure of liberating this amazing little person from your over-stuffed uterus. The reward, of course, is priceless. And for a mother who has just discovered her baby has colic, there is no amount of money she wouldn't pay for a damn good babysitter.

For the first two weeks of her life, my daughter Lainey was a complete angel. Delivered by planned cesarean section, she weighed in at just more than eight pounds. Everything was going according to plan. I was healing well. Lainey was breast-feeding wonderfully, and three-year-old Leah adored her new baby sister. Little did I know this was the calm before the storm. Actually, it was more like the calm before a Category 5 hurricane.

Right when my sweet infant hit the fourteen-day-old mark, she suddenly turned on me. One day, she just started crying—and would not stop. Every attempt at soothing her failed, and I was floored. I didn't know what to do. After all, I thought, I had this mothering stuff down. I had been there and done that before. But, Leah, my first born, would stop crying if I picked her up, held her close, and rocked her. There was never a moment in time, that I can remember, when I was not able to soothe her and get her to stop crying. So what was going on with this new baby?

Clearly, I thought, something was wrong. She had to be struggling with something that I wasn't able to pick up on. As a pharmacist, I knew in the back of my mind that colic could be the cause of her endless cries, but I remained optimistic that after I experimented with a variety of calming techniques, Lainey would eventually calm down. So when she started crying inconsolably, I began performing the series of checks that most new moms know all too well. I first determined she was dry, then moved on down the list: well-fed, adequately burped, and her body temperature was normal. She didn't want to be rocked, held, swaddled, or walked. Nothing I did offered an ounce of relief. After the second day or so of my pulling out my hair, I threw up my hands and took Lainey to the doctor.

When the doctor entered the room, she only had to take one look at me to know I was at my wits' end. My outward appearance was a direct reflection of how I felt on the inside: a complete mess. The black shirt I had on was riddled with spit-up stains, and my beige pants were equally splotchy with remnants of my morning coffee and donut. Once I started talking, my eyes filled up with tears as I began to describe Lainey's every symptom in painstaking detail, from gas to high-pitched shrieks of terror. That's when the doctor looked me in the eye and said, "She probably just has colic. Try lots of white noise and swaddling."

"Just has colic." Those words still stick with me. Saying a baby "just has colic" is like telling someone that your mother-in-law is "just going to move in with you"— permanently, with her five cats. And all the doctor offered for a solution was . . . white noise and swaddling. I just didn't have the energy to tell this woman I'd already tried everything, and nothing had worked. How was I supposed to survive colic? What was I going to do?

I had heard of colic before and knew the repercussions for mommies: ringing ears, frazzled nerves, and a possible divorce lawyer fee. I tried to recall the events leading up to Lainey's first crying spell. "Maybe something is wrong with my breast milk," I thought. "Or maybe it was that broccoli salad I had for lunch. It could have been a hair tourniquet." (This is when one of your hairs gets wrapped around your baby's toe and makes her scream. It happened to my first child. I had read about it before but never imagined it would actually happen!) Other possibilities that you may come up with for your infant's cries may include tiredness, or even teething. True, it would be odd for a two-week-old to sprout a tooth, but hey, you're looking for any possible cause that can be cured, or at least treated!

But no matter what tiny details I tried to retrieve from my tired memory, I couldn't come up with a clear answer. Colic just happens. Some babies, for one reason or another, are meant to begin life's journey by screaming their little lungs out. Maybe they'll grow up to be the next Ozzy Osbourne (don't worry—your odds are pretty slim) or, better yet, a mom. Or, the mom of a baby with colic.

Then, again, maybe I was just having a really bad dream. I told myself this, many times, and actually tried pinching myself. Out of sheer desperation, I even had my three-year-old pinch me, then my husband. When I was about to ask the mailman to pinch me, I knew I had some issues. Thinking back, I should have known it couldn't have been a nightmare. I'd just had a baby—with colic! Sleep . . . what was that?

So, you've been to the doctor. You've ruled out all other possibilities. Your baby has colic. Now what? Please read on.

How to Handle the News

—*Accept it and feel free to complain about it.* You deserve that right. Complain to whomever your little heart desires. Let it out! If you can't find anyone to spill your guts to, grab a pen and paper and vent your frustrations. It was the aftershocks of Lainey's colic that drove me to write. Even after Lainey became better, I was still struggling with the turmoil of it all. Just because she stopped crying so much didn't mean I was fully recovered. Writing turned out to be a very therapeutic way to express my thoughts and concerns without worrying that anyone would pass judgment about me being a bad mommy. And who needs that?

—*Mark it down on the calendar.* Included at the back of this book is a "Colic Countdown Calendar." For every day of colic that you survive, X it out in big bold letters. For every X, you'll earn some sort of prize when the colic days are over. Whether it's a foot massage from your husband or a day of luxury at the local spa, you deserve it.

—*Cry or scream really loudly.* I would often go upstairs, close my bedroom door, and scream. It felt good to get it out. Don't worry if you don't make it to a closed room in time. Your baby will be okay. If you happen to live in an apartment or home where you can hear your own neighbors argue, you can still scream. Maybe they'll have mercy and make dinner for you one night. My point is, it's okay to cry, and it's okay to scream—these are normal reactions to living with a constantly screaming baby.

—*Laugh about it. I call this the laughter response.* Life with colic is sometimes just so absurdly cruel that it becomes funny, and laughing about it helps lighten your load. The best laughs are those from the belly that leave you feeling sore and out of breath. Research has also found that laughter is beneficial to your health and can increase blood flow about as much as some cholesterol-lowering medications and light exercise. Some suggestions for getting a quick laugh include:

- A tickle session with your husband or other children.
- Funny movies: *Something About Mary, Happy Gilmore, A Fish Called Wanda, Airplane!,* and *Coming to America* are a few of my favorites.
- Funny Shows: One you really have to watch, if you haven't already, is *The Ellen Degeneres Show.* Her love for life and quest for happiness is contagious. Other personal favorites include *Seinfeld* reruns, *Scrubs,* and *The Office.*
- Have a "Who can make the silliest face" contest with your other kids.
- Tell your husband you think that you're pregnant.

—*Learn about it.* Read books and surf the Web for colic suggestions. Talk to other mothers who are proud survivors and stay away from those who have perfect babies, at least for the time being. They will only make you feel worse.

—*Tell everyone you know that your baby has colic.* With luck, this will give them plenty of time to volunteer their services when you need to escape.

—*Remember, it really will go away.* It annoyed me when people would say, "Don't worry dear, it will be gone before you know it." "*No it won't!* " I would think to myself. "I know about it every second. When I try to take a shower, eat, or heaven forbid, try to go to the store." Colic seems never ending when you are in the thick of it.

The fact is, though, in most infants, colic really does disappear by the time they hit three or four months. I know it's hard to believe, but that little terror who is now among you will soon be a giggly, drooling, chubby-cheeked little angel. So have faith in yourself. You can handle it. You may often feel yourself teetering between insanity and reason, but most of us, and our babies, make it through unscathed. Remember, you just gave birth to a child— miracles really do happen.

2

Insane in the Membrane

"A child is a curly, dimpled lunatic."
—Ralph Waldo Emerson

ACCORDING TO *WEBSTER'S DICTIONARY*, THE DEFINITION OF insanity is the following: "The state of being insane; derangement of intellect; lunacy."

I think that about sums up what happens to the typical mother by around day two of colic. Looney tooney. You either have to laugh or cry. I chose to laugh and throw two-year-old temper tantrums, which featured me throwing a variety of inanimate objects and cursing every now and then. True, these aren't the healthiest outlets for stress, but they were extremely satisfying. It wasn't until after colic ended that I was able to catch up on healthier alternatives for dealing with an absolute lack of control, decline in judgment, and oh, derangement of intellect.

Let's face it. An inconsolable infant will drive even the best of parents absolutely bonkers. If you feel anything other than totally stressed out, I'd actually wonder if you were human. I mean, how could any woman not go completely crazy in the world of colic?

I bet even Mother Teresa's will would have been tested. And boy, was I a far cry away from the goodness and sanctity of Mother Teresa during my bout with colic. The minute everyone had left my house after a visit, my head would start spinning, and obscenities would start popping out of my mouth. I also learned the art of juggling. It just had nothing to do with balls or fancy gadgets—I juggled an inconsolable infant, a whiny three-year-old, and a deaf dog.

And, I admit, I threw a couple of things. Not at anybody, but at the wall. My poor walls. So, don't feel bad if you happen to throw the remote. It won't be that expensive to replace. Just never hurt yourself or your baby. Remotes can be fixed, and walls can be plastered and painted. That little baby of yours, however, can never be replaced.

Next comes cursing. We all do it. We all regret it. So what do we do about it? Curse, damn it! Just try to go into another room before you begin cursing up a storm. Although your infant has no idea what you are saying, you'll most likely feel guilty for saying the "f" word in front of her. It is for this reason you should at least attempt to avoid exposing her to unnecessary obscenities. There will be times, however, when you just have to let it out and that's okay. I firmly believe the reason babies aren't born with the ability to understand the meaning of words is to protect them. They have no idea what we're muttering. As long as you put that fake smile on your face while cursing up a storm, they won't know the difference.

By the fourth week into colic, I had a hard time containing myself and holding my tongue. My husband, Mike, was working rotating shifts at the beer brewery and never seemed to be home when I was on the verge of a meltdown. Lord knows I could have used a beer! So, I must confess, there were times I said things I shouldn't have. But, I forgive myself, and as far as I know Lainey has no recollection of my not-so-pleasant words. As for Leah, my three-year-old, I always made sure she was not within earshot before I broke out into expletives. All I needed was to get a phone call from her preschool teacher informing me of Leah's use of the phrase "damn it" every time she dropped something. Bottom line: No one is perfect and if it makes you feel a little better to say "oh shit" instead of "oh shoot," go for it.

Now that I've shared what I did to cope, let me offer you some healthier alternatives that may ease your colic days:

−*Meditate.* I just recently started meditating. Thankfully, you don't have to hum and sit crisscross-applesauce style while you do it. Just take five or ten minutes out of your day to do this. Go somewhere quiet (aka, put in earplugs, go in the bedroom and close the door, and turn your fan on high), close your eyes, and focus on your breath. Focus only on your breath going in and your breath going out. Why is this so good? It gives you control of *something.* For that five-minute period, you are controlling how you breathe, and you are relaxed while you do it. It does wonders, trust me. It may be the only thing you have control of all day.

−*Exercise.* I admit it−I am an endorphin junkie. And, when it comes to firing up your body's happy molecules, exercise will make those molecules dance! ! Hard-core exercise is an excellent way to get rid of pent-up stress and help shed some of those extra baby pounds. People at work would ask me how I lost my weight so fast from the pregnancy and my response was, "It was either exercise or a fifth of vodka. I chose the former."

I know what you're thinking: "When in the hell am I supposed to exercise?" and "Yeah right, like I have the energy to exercise with only two hours' sleep in the past five days." Well, I am here to tell you that you must, if physically possible, do something to get your blood flowing. Ask, or beg someone to help with the baby while you work out. Or, join a gym with a trustworthy nursery staff. Some will take infants as young as six weeks old. Trust me ladies, you will feel better after a good thirty-minute workout. Whether you opt for a session of Tae-Bo or a spinning class, your mind and body will both benefit. The hardest part is getting started, but once you get going, you'll be hooked. Hint: Sometimes, just putting on your sneakers and tying up your laces is all it takes to get yourself out the door.

—*Pray.* Prayer does wonders for the soul. Whether you pray to God in heaven or to Buddha, knowing that you can't control everything in your life helps relieve the pressure. The *Book of Psalms* contains scriptures for helping yourself heal and overcoming adversity. If there was ever a time in your life when you needed to ask for the help of God, now is it!

—*Get a massage.* If you can't escape for a half hour to get a professional massage, ask someone close to you for one. Don't be shy. Your husband can be a big help here. I've also started teaching my three-year-old how to give back rubs. You deserve it and need it. Massage helps you relax, even if it's for just fifteen or twenty minutes.

—*Escape.* It's crucial to allow yourself periods to escape from the madness. Whether you have the luxury of physically escaping from home, or if you can settle for a quiet mental escape, it will allow you to regain your sanity. Hand the baby to your husband or partner and announce that it's your time-out period for the next fifteen minutes, half-hour, whatever you need. Hopefully, you're not in this alone, so don't be afraid to ask for help.

. . .

Yes, you will have your moments of madness. Don't feel guilty about it. When you are about to hit rock bottom, beg for a sitter, and run like hell. Just make sure you come back.

3

It Takes a Village

WHATEVER HAPPENED TO THE GOOD OLD DAYS? THE DAYS when streets were occupied with members of your immediate family and, if you needed a hand or a shoulder to cry on, there was always one readily available? Today's families are typically just not as close, in proximity or affection, as they used to be when our parents and grandparents were growing up. Many of us are spread out across the country like wildflowers, and it costs an arm and a leg to fly. Having Grammy nearby to help out with feedings, babysitting, cooking, and cleaning seems like a thing of the past or a remote, albeit great, fantasy.

When you have an inconsolable infant, though, you need all the support you can get. Support in the way of encouragement, or even better, a brief escape outside colic quarters, does wonders for the spirit. So without your immediate family nearby, to whom do you turn?

—In-laws and distant relatives. I don't care how much you may disagree with your mother-in-law, now is the

time to throw your pride out the window and allow her to take control. If she'll watch the baby for you so that you can escape to run errands, let her reorganize your cabinets, if that's what makes her happy. Do you have an aunt you intentionally avoid sitting next to at holiday gatherings because she smells like mothballs? Call her. Invite her over, and ask her for help. Your nose will survive, and your nerves will thank you.

—*Husband/partner.* Let's not forget that often there's another body in the house who's there for more than sharing a meal with you and doing a few loads of laundry. Sure, he may work hard during the day (or at night, if you've got yourself a midnight warrior) but you have a full-time job yourself. And you don't get to take a lunch break or even enjoy the peaceful ride to work. So, when your hubby does come home, ask him for help. You need, and deserve, some alone time.

—*Friends.* If you're an extravert and have plenty of girlfriends to call for support and help, then you are way ahead of where I was when I had Lainey. Until recently, I always considered myself an introvert. I usually had a few close friends whom I talked to now and again (my husband affectionately refers to me as the "anti-woman" since I hate talking on the phone and shopping). But I never called on the few friends I had to help when I was in colic hell. Silly, in retrospect, but I didn't want to impose and then feel bad for asking since I hadn't talked to some of them in a while. After surviving colic, I now know how important it is to build and nurture those relationships. Whether you prefer phone or e-mail, try to keep connected with your closest friends, and don't pretend to be Superwoman! It is when you admit you are less than perfect to your friends that your relationships blossom. Admit when you need their help, and you'll likely be able to return the favor one day.

—*Neighbors.* Once upon a time, neighbors were almost always your friends. Whether you needed to borrow a cup of sugar or ask for their assistance in moving your refrigerator, you could always rely on them. Nowadays, few of us seem to have neighbors we know really well, if at all. But having a colicky baby should inspire you to get to know them, and know them well! They can turn out to be lifesavers. When one of my neighbors invited my three-year-old over for a play date during one of Lainey's bad days, I was ecstatic! It was just the reprieve I needed. So, if you're fortunate enough to be surrounded by wonderful, trustworthy neighbors, take full advantage of their hospitality.

—*Your church.* Wouldn't it be great if God himself could make a temporary appearance in your family room and offer his assistance for an hour or so while you escape? In lieu of that, ask your fellow church members for numbers of responsible sitters; these same members may offer up their own babysitting services. Let them know your baby has colic, and compare it to living in hell. They'll get the picture.

—*Local playgroups/mom groups.* There are hundreds of support groups for mothers online and, most likely, in your very own town. It helps to vent your frustrations to other moms who can share that "been there, done that" insight. I've included some of the more popular, nationally recognized groups at the back of the book (see Appendix II).

—*Area Social Services.* Your local Social Services department can provide you with a variety of parenting support options available in your community. Many also offer free parenting classes at no cost to you.

—*Professionals.* You can always turn to a professional for help. Also in Appendix II is a list of some important hot-line numbers and Web sites. Your primary care doctor, obstetrician, and even your baby's pediatrician are all good starting points for seeking help.

—*Nanny Services.* There will be times when you have to search for help from people you may not know in order to gain a few glimpses of sanity. A professional nanny or licensed childcare provider may just be your saving grace, if you can afford it. Just remember to proceed with caution: There are good nannies, and there are bad nannies. Most are wonderful, capable, and loving individuals, who are devoted to raising your child in the best light possible, but it's imperative to check out references prior to hiring someone to help with your new baby. Ask your friends and coworkers for nanny references or childcare referrals. You can also check online, in the local newspaper, and in your phonebooks for licensed nanny services in your area.

...

If you're staying at home full-time with your colicky baby (and there's room in your budget), having someone who can take the baby while you take some alone time and/or time away with your other children can help you recharge. Whether it's for a day a week or twice a month, you will appreciate the break, and it will be well worth the money. Also, try to plan for at least a couple date nights with your husband or significant other each month. This is where your colic countdown calendar comes in (see Appendix IV). It helps remind you to book a babysitter since you have so many other things on your mind right now. My husband and I were not able to go out alone until Lainey was about six weeks old, and by that time I was really going crazy. If I had been able to plan a little better, we would have ventured out a lot sooner.

Even attending a good sporting event with your hubby will offer you some peace and quiet compared to what you're currently living with! For those who aren't that into sports, I highly recommend a good old-fashioned dinner and a movie night. It's so nice to be able to sit still for more than one minute and enjoy a freshly prepared seafood platter and dessert of your choice. And, to top it off, it will all be served in a peaceful, kid-free environment. Oh, you will also appreciate the adult conversation offered by your husband.

Please, I beg of you, do not be afraid to ask for help—as long as you know whom you are asking. It is in your baby's best interest that you do so. Embrace your friends, family, and neighbors, and start looking early on, even before you give birth if possible, for high-quality, paid help, just in case no one else is around and you are in desperate need of a break.

4

Everyone Hates Me
(and I'm No Good)

I DON'T HAVE ENOUGH FINGERS AND TOES TO COUNT HOW many people I believed hated me during Lainey's colic months. After divulging my state of maternal helplessness and neediness to those around me, I still couldn't fathom why no one offered to put their life on hold to become my live-in nanny. What was wrong with these people? Did they just not get it, or what? Between the evil glares, rude comments, and worthless suggestions for quieting my baby, you would have thought I had a sign around my neck that stated, "I am an idiot and have no clue what I am doing."

And it's every mommy's worst fear, isn't it? That the rest of the world will discover she has no idea how to calm her own child.

But looking back, it's a wonder that I managed as well as I did. In the box, "A Day in the Life," I've outlined how my typical day might have played out.

A DAY IN THE LIFE

5:01 a.m. Both of my girls wake up. Three-year-old wants to play Hide and Seek. I say no, she cries and says I am not her friend.

5:15 a.m. Husband wakes up. I ask him to help with the baby so I can shower. He say's, "Sorry, running late for work."

He has no time to help me, and he gets to escape to work–the nerve!

6:30 a.m. The sun is out. With my PJs on, and Leah in an outfit she hand selected herself, we decide to go outside for a stroll. A bird flies too close to the stroller. Lainey starts wailing. Neighbor peers out of her window and looks at me as if I am the Antichrist. Why she isn't running out to help I have no idea. We are up to three on the "Who Hates Me" list today.

10:01 a.m. Work up enough courage to go to the store–I am out of breast pads. Once Lainey is fastened in her car seat, she screams bloody murder for the entire trip. Leah asks for earplugs. Fellow drivers cut me off, jump in front of me at red lights. I roll down my windows to get even.

10:20 a.m. We arrive at Target, and everyone is now completely stressed out. After I calm Lainey down, we enter the store, and the bright lights and unfamiliar faces make her very mad. She screams. Once I get to the baby section to look for breast pads, I'm greeted by other moms with their quietly sleeping infants in tow, all peering at me out of the corners of their eyes, as if they're better than me at this mothering thing. In the check-out line, Lainey continues to cry and the clerk feels compelled to tell me that her niece was colicky and she didn't grow out of it until she was one-year-old. "Gee,

continued

thanks. That's just what I wanted to hear!" I don't think she likes my comment. Oh, well.

11 a.m. My friend Susan arrives when Lainey is in one of her fits. My irritable mood is obvious and becomes even worse when Susan starts asking the typical stupid questions everyone asks, such as "Do you think she is hungry? Is she sick?" No, no, and please shut the hell up! Of course, I don't say this, but I sure do feel like it and think she can tell. Oops.

1:30 p.m. Realize we have no milk or dinner so we head off to the grocery store. Of course, Lainey starts to cry after being in the store all of one minute and then the comments and looks start rolling in. There is the lady behind the deli counter and the grandmother waiting for her thinly sliced turkey. I think they both catch me rolling my eyes as they offer their suggestions for the cries, but they still just keep right on talking . . . and talking, and Lainey's screams are getting louder . . . and louder.

5 p.m. Crap! I forgot to get dinner when I was at the grocery store and have to order pizza. I greet the delivery lady with a screaming baby in my arms. She courageously remarks, "Maybe she's hungry, too. Have you tried feeding her lately?" Oh, the things I wanted to say and do at that moment!

6 p.m. Husband gets home from work. I do the Lainey hand-off and call my mom to tell her about my horrible day. I also tell my brother who happens to be at her house. None of them offers to come help me, and she only lives an hour away. I decide they're getting really bad Christmas presents.

8 p.m. At the same time, I'm trying to read my three-year-old a much-deserved goodnight story, Mike enters her room with Lainey squealing and attacking his chest hairs.

continued

Even though I've just finished nursing her, I know that she wants more. Leah has a tantrum and tells me I'm not her friend, again.

8:30 p.m. Time for my first attempt at sleep. Husband asks for sex and I, of course, say, Hell no! He just has no clue.

So, the days would start with people hating me and end with the same. Here's my list of my less-than-fans for the day:

1. Leah
2. Mike
3. Neighbor
4. Man in blue Toyota
5. Lady in red Mustang
6. Mother in yellow shirt with sleeping baby
7. Pregnant mother in sundress with four-year-old
8. The Target cashier
9. Susan
10. Grocery deli clerk
11. Grandma at grocery store
12. Pizza delivery lady
13. Leah
14. Mike
15. Oh, and the whole time, Lainey

So, in a matter of fifteen hours, I had an equal number of meetings with people who thought I was either mean or just plain inept. No, I did not take a mothering course, but I read a lot of books, thumbed through plenty of magazines, and surfed the Internet for parenting tips. What did the world expect from me?

It will be only after the colic ends that you'll realize you probably took some things a little too personally. For instance, that guy who cut you off this morning could have been on his way to witness the birth of his first baby. Your neighbor, who you thought was scowling at you, was actually an insomniac who just happened to be looking out the window when you passed by. And, as for your colicky baby, well, she loves you more than ever.

I know how insecure caring for an inconsolable infant can make you feel. But give yourself some credit, and take what other people say with a grain of salt. Right now, you just need to focus on how you can reach beneath your belly flab, pull out that last remnant of gusto you have left, and learn how to make it through another day.

5

Sweet Escape

*"The taste of chocolate is a sensual pleasure in itself,
existing in the same world as sex. . . . For myself, I can enjoy
the wicked pleasure of chocolate . . . entirely by myself.
Furtiveness makes it better."* —Dr. Ruth Westheimer

AS YOU WILL SOON FIND OUT (OR MAY ALREADY KNOW), IT'S
always when you seem to be having the worst day of your
life that not a soul is around to help. Moments like these
require that you turn to a most trusted friend and
confidant. And for me, the one that has always been there
through thick and thin is chocolate.

Chocolate is a popular endorphin booster. Its consumption is associated with feelings of happiness, con-
tentment, and satisfaction. A good, quality chocolate is
sweet in taste, velvety in texture, and melts in your mouth.
What's more, consuming it is not only extremely grati-
fying but may even be good for you. According to the journal *Hypertension*, the antioxidants found in dark chocolate could help reduce bad cholesterol and blood pressure.
As to how much a person needs to consume in order to
reap the benefits, the results are still pending. But the
mere suggestion adds credibility, at least to my mind, to
the importance of my periodic chocolate time-outs.

For all of you breast-feeding moms, don't despair. You, too, can eat the almighty chocolate bar. It is well known in the medical community that large amounts of caffeine can contribute to the irritability of infants. And milk and dark chocolate both contain caffeine. But the good news is that there are a lot of chocolate products that contain minimal amounts of caffeine, especially when compared to other products that you may readily consume. For instance, one cup of coffee contains approximately 100 mg of caffeine, although the numbers vary widely. A normal cup of decaffeinated coffee still has 2 to 3 mg of caffeine per cup, and a glass of tea has anywhere from 20 to 90 mg of caffeine per cup. Now, compare these numbers with that of one Hershey's chocolate bar: 9 mg of caffeine. That's it! Even better, a KitKat has only 6 mg of caffeine, and Skor toffee bars contain a mere 3 mg of caffeine. And to wash it all down, a glass of chocolate milk using 2 tablespoonfuls of chocolate syrup only has about 6 mg of caffeine.

So, when consumed responsibly, you can take advantage of the powers of chocolate without guilt. For all of you dark chocolate lovers out there, you should probably note that it contains an average of three times more caffeine than its milk chocolate counterpart. White chocolate contains a minimal amount, if any. In Appendix IV, you will find a "Chocoholic's Caffeine Content Guide" to assist you in your chocolate-eating endeavors.

For the formula feeders, have at it!

There is, of course, a right way and a wrong way to consume chocolate. Just to make sure you obtain the full benefits of your chocolate experience, here are some important rules to follow:

—*Rule #1: Set the scene.* Never eat chocolate with a screaming baby in hand. Why ruin your special chocolate moment with someone screaming in your ear? Try to go someplace quiet—are you laughing? I thought so. Well, believe it or not, it is possible to go somewhere a little quiet; it just involves a closed door, the use of earplugs, and a fan or two.

A CHOCOLATE ESCAPE

Here's what I did when Lainey entered one of her nonstop cry cycles:

I would place her safely in her crib, sprint to the kitchen, frantically toss around a couple bags of chocolate assortments until I found just the right piece, and high-tail it to my bedroom. I'd close the door (okay, I usually slammed it), insert earplugs, turn my fan on turbo power, and consume. I would close my eyes and imagine my special happy place, a land inhabited only by loving, non-whiny people with crystal blue waters and a never-ending supply of piña coladas.

After a few minutes of perpetual bliss, I would venture back out and try to console my screaming baby.

—*Rule #2: Don't overdo it.* I know it's difficult, but you can only allow yourself a few minutes in a chocolate time-out for the pure sake of your waistline. Too much time alone sets the stage for the consumption of very large amounts of chocolate. I always found it best to use my "ration bowl," as my husband calls it, a tiny round bowl large enough for only a handful of munchies or approximately six Hershey's kisses. I have no self-control, so I would never have dared to escape with a full bag of chocolates. Maybe you can, but some chocoholics are not so lucky.

—*Rule #3: Never feel guilty about it.* You're entitled to your periodic sweet escapes. These moments allow you to enjoy something you like for a little while and provide you with a temporary break from the cries. If you do by some slim chance go overboard and eat much more chocolate than you should, you can always expend those extra calories by partaking in one of my favorite stress relievers: slam dancing in the family room or walking like a mad woman on a treadmill.

6

I Think I Can

MOTHER TERESA ONCE SAID, "I KNOW GOD WILL NOT GIVE ME anything I can't handle. I just wish that He didn't trust me so much." Well ladies, God must think mighty highly of you to deliver unto you a constantly screaming infant, right? I honestly believe that all mothers of chronically fussy babies were carefully selected for this daunting task. It is not by chance that you have such a special baby, but it is because you possess an inner strength and will to survive, which is found only in a select group of individuals.

One of my favorite stories growing up was about the little engine that could. I don't know how many times I called upon that popular tale to keep me going, but I can think of a few:

- I think I can take a shower before the baby wakes up
- I think I can lose ten pounds (I would repeat this over and over in hopes of tricking my fat cells into spontaneously combusting)

- I think I can squeeze into my non-maternity jeans
- I think I can sleep for a four-hour stretch
- I think I can take my baby to the mall so I can go clothes shopping

Here are some more realistic "I think I cans" in colic land:

- I think I can use the bathroom with the baby on my lap
- I think I can lose my double chin I've gotten from all the awkward facial expressions I've been making
- I think I can eat dinner in peace when my kids are in college
- I think I can go shopping if equipped with more than two dozen items, including four pacifiers, a rattle, the barnyard book, a squeaky duck, a stroller mobile, three changes of clothes (one for me), five diapers, a pack of wipes, and, I know I'm forgetting something—

But, really:

You can survive this.

I mean, think about it. There are probably dozens of events that you can recollect in your life that you never thought you would survive. One particular event I can remember is my trip to summer camp in North Carolina at the ripe age of thirteen. Horribly homesick, I cried every night for the first few days. We slept in these things called hogans, which are, basically, covered wagons without the wheels. The beds consisted of a wooden base with a thin mattress on top, my sleeping bag, and a pillow. There was no air-conditioning, there were no doors, and there was a roof made of durable cloth. It was nothing like the comforts of home.

I felt so alone in this primitive campsite and thought I'd never get home soon enough. Then came the night of the campout in the field. As if the hogans weren't bad enough, the counselors deemed it necessary to move all of us out into a mosquito field for a giant sleepover. As I curled up in my sleeping bag with a couple of crickets, I gazed up at the beautiful summer sky. The stars sparkled wildly and the crescent-shaped moon hovered directly over my fluorescent-green sleeping bag. In the distance, I could hear leaves rustling, owls hooting, and teenage boys engaged in a burping contest. I suddenly felt at one with nature, and, despite being out in the great wide open, I felt amazingly secure and content. Around me were about thirty other kids, some quite shameless, mind you, and above me were the nightlights of nature.

I think that night aged my sense of confidence and humbleness by about two decades. Never in a million years did I think I could sleep outside, in the dark, without my mom and dad or a tent, and not have a nervous breakdown. But, I did it—I survived. And the rest of my week at camp was pure joy and excitement.

Things do normally happen for a reason. All the other things you've gotten through so far in life have prepared you for your role as a mother and colic survivor. Even though it may be hard right now to grasp the fact that in the next couple months or so, your miserable infant will soon be a big ball of fun, just remember the little engine that did.

SECTION TWO
Mommy Survival 101
How to Take Care of You

Only mothers who learn how to take care of themselves are capable of caring for a cranky, irritable infant. For you frequent flyers out there, you've all heard the flight attendant's speech on what to do in case the oxygen masks deploy. They always remind parents of young children to put the mask on themselves before they place it over their child. This is because a dead parent is of no help, right? Makes sense.

So, why is it so hard for mothers on land to realize that they, too, need to survive? We have to eat, sleep, provide our families with shelter, and shower once in a while. And, in order to accomplish any of these necessities, we will have to sometimes let our babies cry. Trust me, I know the worst sounds in the world to a new mother are her baby's cries. But once you have done everything humanly possible to help soothe your infant, that's when you *have to take a step back and accept that your baby is going to cry, <u>no matter what you do</u>. What you can do to help your child is to ensure that you are well taken care of. Without meeting your needs, it's impossible to meet your baby's. This section is devoted to helping you accomplish this difficult task.*

Get ready, get set . . .

7

I'm Starving

I FIND IT IRONIC THAT MOTHERS SPEND A LARGE PORTION OF their days supplying their children with food and drink, yet these same children make it impossible for us mothers to eat. Sometimes you just plain forget to eat. But most of the time you really want, so very badly, to sit down for five minutes and eat something that requires heat to cook it. For me, that was a dream.

When my daughter had colic, on any given day, I could be seen pacing about my kitchen. I entered the kitchen quite frequently, but I usually forgot why. I would try really hard to think why I had gone in there. Was it for a glass of water? Or was it a pacifier? "Oh, hell," I thought, "I'll just grab both."

Right when I was about to clench something in my hand, the baby would wake up, or someone would look at her the wrong way, and she would erupt into one of her episodes. I would leap from the kitchen, wondering what was wrong, as if something actually were. There never was.

She would just be sitting there, in her seat, spitting nails for no apparent reason. Then I'd have to wonder, what was I doing again? By about the tenth hour of running to and fro like a human yo-yo, I would begin to hear something strange—a rumbling sound of sorts. And out of nowhere, I would hear it. That loud, thunderous voice crying out, day after day: "FEEEEED MEEEEE," it exclaimed. The pits of my belly were shouting for help.

I finally realized it was food I was searching for all day. That would explain my crankiness, forgetfulness, and sometimes-delusional state, which, by the way, are all symptoms of low blood sugar (and motherhood). After experiencing long episodes of hunger and hypoglycemia during my colic days, I found the four biggest obstacles to eating were:

1. Getting to the food
2. Figuring out which food
3. Cooking the food, and
4. Eating the food

To the typical adult, the above obstacles seem like simple enough tasks to complete, but to the colic mom, they are anything but easy. Trips to the grocery store with a screaming infant, deciding what to buy, turning on a stove, and eating with one hand take lots of practice, and patience, to perfect.

GETTING TO THE FOOD

The food that kind people deliver to the homes of new parents usually disappears by day two. After eating all of your stored batches of lasagna, you soon realize that you eventually have to make a trip with your new baby to the grocery store for a cabinet replenishment ceremony. She, however, suddenly makes it impossible to do so. It is not just that she is screaming and won't stop; it is that you know there is nothing you can do about it, and you don't want to subject innocent shoppers to these horrific sounds.

So what do you do?

Here's what I did: I stalled. I starved for a few days. Then my husband started complaining. I ignored him. But when Leah, my three-year-old, actually began asking for food and I had to say, "Sorry, honey, we don't have that" or "Nope, no pretzels, how about okra?" I knew I had no choice. I could get by on next to nothing—after all, I had that baby fat to lose. And my husband, he could fend for himself. And wasn't that a little tire I saw around his waist this morning? But my little girl? Her, I could not neglect.

I would have sent Mike to the store if given the opportunity. He, however, was working insane hours and did not happen to be home when I finally realized we were in dire need of food that wasn't moldy or freezer burnt.

So, finally, I went. I said screw it, and just went. Upon our ear-piercing entrance, I was met with looks of pity and disappointment. Every single person in that grocery store was staring and, as anxiety-provoking as that is in itself, they did not do so quietly. Oh, no. First, they whispered to each other. Then, they chimed in with their little words of advice and continued to express their deepest sympathy for my poor squealing baby:

"Oh, the poor thing. Do you think she's hungry?"
My response: "Oh no, she just ate!"

What I wanted to say: "Do I look like a total idiot?
Take this grapefruit and shove it."

"Wow, someone is not very happy, is she!"
My response: A condescending stare.
What I wanted to say: "No kidding, lady! With all of
your genius, you should try out for Jeopardy!*"*

"My grandmother used to give me a little splash of
whiskey to help me calm down when I was a baby."
My response: "Really?"
What I wanted to say: "And maybe that is why you
should know when to keep your mouth shut! Now,
close it and move your little alcoholic self out of
my way."

Clearly, I had a few colic-induced rage issues to work
out. But just so you know, I do not like to be the center
of attention. I would rather be the girl in the background
whom no one notices right away. Well, I knew then and
there that those days were over, and to make matters
worse, not one single person asked how *I* was doing!
What was wrong with these people? I decided never to
face that kind of scrutiny again.

But what choice did I have? It turns out, plenty. It's just
that in my head-ringing, sleep-deprived brain, I didn't realize what those choices were. That's why I'm laying it all
out for you here.

Order Online if Possible

Seems obvious. We've known about Fresh Direct, Peapod,
and Netgrocer for years. But if you're outside of their

delivery zone, or you don't want to pay their hefty delivery fees, you're out of luck. Well, not exactly. It turns out many local grocery stores offer an Internet express shopping method where you can order your items online and just go pick them up. The fee is usually very small, and many stores offer it free with high-dollar orders. This is a beautiful thing. No check-out line. Run in, run out. You'll be gone before your baby's screams even hit the cash registers.

Enlist Your Husband's Help

If your husband is home and able, hand him the grocery list. Keep in mind that you need to be as specific as possible if he doesn't normally do the shopping. For instance, don't just write down "diapers." Be sure to specify the size and preferred brand, or he is likely to return with Pull-Ups fit for a toddler rather than the Pampers Swaddlers you desired.

Buy in Bulk

Save your money and sanity by purchasing items in bulk. It's well worth it to pay a small membership fee (usually around $40) to join the local Sam's Club or Costco. What this means: fewer trips to the store. That's clear. But what you might not know: These clubs sell their stuff in WAREHOUSES! Do you realize how huge those places are? It's amazing. You rarely, if ever, come face-to-face with another shopper. So Lainey's screams could barely be heard two aisles over. And if someone actually did hear her peals of thunder, they had no idea where they were coming from. No one could truly point the finger at us. Checking out was a little tougher, but it was a small price to pay for two whole months of supplies!

Shop When No One Is Watching

We live in the age of twenty-four-hour grocery stores. This a wonderful modern convenience for us mothers. Although I would always attempt sleeping when the rest of the world was, there were many nights I was not able to. So here's what I did—whenever Lainey was having one of her "I refuse to go back to sleep" nights, I would strap her in her car seat and head off to the store. Why not take advantage of this time when my husband was home asleep and I could at least leave my three-year-old home in bed. And, the only other shoppers that happened to be out were either too drunk or too tired to notice my little screamer. Just make sure you drive defensively.

FIGURING OUT WHICH FOOD

Deciding what food to buy is a lot more complex than you might imagine. There are many factors to consider, such as whether or not you like your dinners hot or cold and how easy it is to eat these meals one-handed. And, since you're probably a little forgetful these days, it's in your best interest to take out your pen and paper and do this figuring at home. If you dare head to the store without a list, you will most likely come home with a case of beer, a bag of chips, and some Tylenol. Also, add this to your list: paper plates, lots of them. Don't worry about the trees or the landfill right now—you deserve this one luxury, if only temporarily. Taking all these points into consideration, I came up with some helpful meal-specific suggestions:

Breakfast

This is one of the easiest meals to buy for. Although you may be thinking cereal is a good choice, unless you are like my father-in-law who soaks his cereal in milk for a good thirty minutes before eating it, don't bother. You will end up with a bowl of mush! Some good choices:

—*Cereal bars.* You can eat them on the go and with one hand. There are several to choose from and most are fortified with extra vitamins.

—*Bagels.* A bagel and cream cheese can hang out on the coffee table a good couple hours or so before going bad. Just watch out for the dog.

—*Yogurt.* Very good for you. Just eat quickly because it spoils fast and tastes horrible at room temperature. Yogurt drinks are also a great choice. You can sip away and feed baby at the same time.

—*Fresh fruit.* You can't go wrong with fresh apples or bananas. Be careful with eating anything too juicy with baby in hand such as oranges or grapefruit. Your baby is liable to get a shot of OJ in the eye—not a good colic calmer.

Lunch and Dinner

A good rule of thumb is this: If you can find one package that provides more than one of the four food groups, buy it. Some of my lunch and dinner favorites include the following:

—*Birds Eye Voila's.* They come in chicken and shrimp varieties and normally include a vegetable and carbohydrate (pasta or rice). I like to mix in extra frozen veggies such as peas or broccoli and I usually add some extra angel hair to the pasta meals.

—*Frozen lasagna.* Two of my favorites are chicken and vegetable lasagna. If you want to get really fancy, you can add a salad (from a bag) and breadsticks!

—*Lean Cuisines.* When it comes to convenience, these win first prize. Not only are they low in fat, but they're also pleasing to the palate. Most of these meals cook in less than five minutes and are relatively healthy. They also now come in bigger portion sizes so you can actually eat one and not still be starving. The grilled paninis are tasty and quite filling when you add some pretzels on the side. Just watch out for the sodium content if you have any blood pressure issues. Although these products are normally good for the waistline, any foods that are high in sodium can cause unwanted fluid retention as well.

—*Pizza.* You don't have to feel guilty about eating pizza anymore. There are many low-fat varieties out there. Some go in the microwave and some still require the oven. One of the best things about pizza is you can eat it with one hand, and it also tastes good cold.

—*Pre-made salads.* From pasta salad to chicken salad, buying something already made at the deli and ready to eat is nice. You also never have to worry about it getting cold!

—*Dessert.* This is my favorite meal of the day, and there are plenty of choices in this category. Whether you are a fellow chocoholic or a health nut, there are colic compatible choices to pick from. Brownies, cookies, and chocolate bars can be easily eaten with one hand, and you can leave them sitting out for hours with no issues. If you're trying to eat healthily, try frozen yogurt or strawberries topped with Cool Whip.

COOKING THE FOOD

If you're eager to impress someone with your culinary skills, now is not the time. However, if you're seeking revenge, cooking for them in the midst of all this could be quite rewarding! It still amazes me that in those early months with Lainey, not once did I ever have to call the fire department. I came pretty close, though. When trying to broil some chicken breasts, I quickly realized that chicken, with a dash of white wine, could easily catch fire when left unattended for more than an hour under the broiler. Luckily my husband saw the smoke and saved the day. After that, I just made sure I knew where my fire extinguisher was at all times and tried to keep my three-year-old out of the kitchen when I was cooking. Here are some tips to help ensure your home will still be standing after three months:

—*Do not cook anything requiring quick reaction times.* This includes broiling something in the oven, blackening, and, of course, flambéing. No, I have never flambéed, but I have watched it on TV, and it looks pretty dangerous.

—*Break out your slow cooker.* A slow cooker is about the easiest way to ensure your family ends up with some sort of meal without too much risk involved. Just throw in some pork or chicken, carrots, potatoes, and seasoning, and eat whenever you can. If you like Indian food, try this: Pour in one jar of your favorite store-bought Indian curry sauce, one package chicken breast, and one can of peas into your crock pot. After four hours on low, pour over some microwavable basmati rice or couscous. It's wonderful—and healthy!

—*Less is best.* I admit, I once tried to cook a four-course meal to prove to myself I could do it. I thought I had it all planned out. Lainey was asleep, my oldest was watching a show, and the dog was content. Of course, upon turning the oven on, all hell broke loose. The dog started barking, Lainey woke up, Leah was bored with her show, and both of the girls started crying in unison. It seems to happen that way. Keep it simple.

—*Microwave your way to happiness.* If your meal comes with directions for the microwave then, by all means, nuke it. Why? There will be less chance of disaster. As long as you punch in the right numbers, you're home free.

As you can see, the theme of this chapter is ease—easy food and going easy on yourself. Even if you're normally a three-star chef, now is not the time to show off. Even if you had visions of keeping your house organic or vegan or pure in some other way, now is not the time. If your husband asks to bring his out-of-town clients home to sample your famous coq au vin, you can tell him now is definitely not the time (unless they like macaroni and cheese out of the box served on plastic ware).

EATING THE FOOD

If your baby is like most colicky infants, dinnertime is a washout. By that time of the day, you're most likely starving for a good meal and your baby is most likely screaming her little head off, very loudly, with no end in sight. Here's what you do:

—*Cut up your food first as if you are serving it to a child.* It is next to impossible to cut up your food and hold a screaming baby at the same time. By cutting it ahead of time, you can eat with one hand and hold the baby with the other.

—*Avoid sharp utensils.* One of the only things that helped ensure that I ate dinner was to place Lainey face down on my lap and bounce her. This is easier said than done. As you jiggle and jostle, the path to your mouth becomes treacherous. And frankly, forks hurt when they stab you in the lip. Spoons come in handy, and so do your fingers.

—*Use plastic cups.* Glasses will break, and water will spill. It's hard to balance a violently screaming baby on your lap while taking a sip of water. Since we will all try this daring move, it is best to avoid the use of anything that may break and spray sharp, projectile objects around you and your new baby.

—*Prepare your dining room.* Strategically placed around me at dinnertime were a baby swing, a bouncy seat, a baby carrier, and countless toys. My dining experience was akin to a chess game—I planned every move with careful thought and calculation. I would usually start with the swing. Sometimes it would work for a few minutes. After that, I would try the bouncy seat with music, then add vibration if needed. When that didn't work, I tried music, no vibration, and lights. When that failed, I tried no music, no lights, and only vibration. I think you get the point. You spend all your time trying to appease this little creature, and you never get to eat! What I usually resorted to, after trying everything under the sun, was the belly bounce—not very enjoyable while eating, but it allowed a couple minutes of conversation among the rest of my family and allowed me to put food into my mouth.

Truly, the sound of a crying infant is a gut-wrenching experience. Add hunger to the list and your stomach is tied in knots. The good news is if you can survive an inconsolable infant for three months, you can do anything. Whether you want to climb Mount Everest or become the next contestant on *Survivor: Motherland*, once you get through the current chaos, anything is possible.

8

The Walking Zombie

"Everyone should have kids. They are the greatest joy in the world. But they are also terrorists. You'll realize this as soon as they are born and they start using sleep deprivation to break you." —Ray Romano, *Everything and a Kite*

WAS IT JUST ME OR DO YOU ALSO SCARE THE SOCKS OFF THE neighborhood children? Do they see you, drop their balls, and run for cover?

And, do you by chance whip out your left boob in the middle of the street and offer it to your wailing infant as cars go by?

I was never sure if it was my outward appearance or the chance of someone catching a glimpse of my giant areola that frightened my neighbors every time I ventured out for a stroll. Whatever the reasons, I hold no grudges. I know I looked like death warmed over. My hair was normally bundled up into some odd shape resembling a rodent, and my frozen, expressionless face was hardly inviting.

Why was I such a mess? I kept forgetting to look in the mirror! You see, when you are sleep deprived, your brain is not operating at normal speed. Simple tasks become undoable, and getting from point A to point B is like swimming across the Atlantic Ocean and back. You start out okay, and then you just keep drifting off, and you end up floating aimlessly about.

For me, sleep was a dream in itself. My husband went back to work full-time when Lainey was two weeks old. Right when colic set in, he was out the door. He had to rotate day, afternoon, and the midnight shifts at the brewery so he was a mess in his own right. My in-laws had gone back to Buffalo, my mom went back to work, and I was all alone with my newborn and three-year-old. I was not a happy camper.

If your baby is anything like Lainey, you will relate to the following torturous scenario that seemed to happen pretty much every night at our house:

You have just nursed your baby to sleep. The time is 10 p.m., and you are on your third attempt at laying her down for the night. Very cautiously, you tiptoe your way towards the bassinet and gently lay her down. You can feel your heart beating out of your chest as you question whether baby is actually going to fall asleep or if she is going through one of her growth spurts and wants to nurse every thirty minutes. "Should I or should I not try to sleep just yet? She looked tired and full enough. Okay, I will try it again." So, you get nice and snuggled under the covers and close your eyes. Right about the same time, you hear her grunt and rustle. You open your eyes and see the bassinet jiggle. Then you begin to pray, really hard, that she will sleep for at least two to three hours. It seems to have worked. She quiets, your eyes close, and off to dreamland you go. As you are just about to take a sip of your frozen strawberry daiquiri

while basking in the Caribbean sun, you are inter-
rupted by your baby's cries. Your baby is up! "No sleep
for you!" the sleep Nazi shouts, or at least you
thought you heard it. And this cycle tends to repeat
itself in a very unpredictable fashion until you feel
you are going to go cuckoo.

So, how can you get more sleep?

—*Take a Nap.* If you are lucky enough to have friends and relatives close by who offer their assistance, then invite them over during the day while you take a two- to three-hour nap. Don't worry about playing hostess. They will, or should, understand! If no one is available, then try to pick two or three different times for your nap attempts. If you try to nap every time your baby does, you will never sleep. First of all, you most likely have other things you have to do, and you just don't have enough time in the day to sleep as much as your baby. Secondly, unless you're a human sleep machine, it is physically impossible for an adult to fall asleep at precisely the same moment as your infant. So, pick a time in the early morning and afternoon. Believe it or not, one or two fifteen-minute power naps can really help you feel better.

—*Shift Work.* At night, if your husband is available, try to do shift work with the baby. If breast-feeding, it is in your best interest to offer your baby a bottle of breast milk given to her by your husband when they are around two weeks old. Not only will this allow your husband to bond with the baby, but it will also allow you some shuteye. If your husband has to work, and works a normal day shift from about 9 a.m. to 5 p.m., then perhaps the best time for him to have baby duty would be the 8 p.m. to midnight shift. This would allow you a solid four-hour stretch of sleep. If you are not breast-feeding, by all means, go down at 6 or 7 p.m. If you are breast-feeding, though, you'll probably find it hard to go more than four hours before becoming drenched in your own breast milk.

Here are some other tricks:

- For daytime naps, do not sleep in the same room as the baby because you will wake up with every toss and turn. Just bring the monitor with you or keep an ear out for the cries.
- Some mothers enjoy co-sleeping with their infants. While this works for many moms and their babies, it has also resulted in tragedy. Babies have suffocated to death when one of their parents rolls over on them during sleep. Mothers seem to possess a heightened sense of awareness, even during sleep, of their baby's whereabouts, more so than the father. But still, co-sleeping with your baby is never without risk. This is a decision only you can make.
- Keep rooms bright during the day and dimly lit at night. I also highly recommend room-darkening shades for baby's room.
- If breastfeeding, avoid products with a high caffeine content after lunchtime. This is where Appendix IV, the "Chocoholic's Guide to Caffeine," will come in handy.

As a pharmacist, I believe all new babies should be stamped with a warning sticker on their foreheads similar to the ones you find on prescription narcotics:

Warning: May cause drowsiness. Alcohol may inten-
sify this effect. Use CAUTION when operating a car
or heavy machinery.

And I would further caution you to avoid the following specific events:

- driving cars, or bikes for that matter, for long dis-
tances
- assembling strollers or walkers
- attempting to learn a new trade that requires the
use of anything sharp or motorized

• • •

Babies make us tired. Period. Whether they sleep like
little angels (highly doubtful in the beginning) or keep you
up into the wee hours of the night, their high level of needs
will most likely cloud your judgment. But have faith. In
just a couple of months, their smiles will undoubtedly lead
you to their sparkling silver lining.

9

What Smells?

MY MOST DIFFICULT TASK AFTER LAINEY'S BIRTH WAS NOT picking out shirts that hid my circular breast pads or even figuring out how to stop her from crying. My most difficult task was taking a shower in peace. And, as for a relaxing bubble bath, I never would have even tried unless my husband was home and on Valium. If only I knew then how beneficial a bath could actually be, or how much better I would smell after a two-minute shower, I would have plunged in a lot sooner.

There are two possible explanations for why mothers of colicky and fussy infants tend to fall below the curve in their hygiene levels:

Reason #1
You just forget. Leave it to a three-year-old to politely ask the question, "Mommy, what smells?" When Leah asked me this innocent question, I wanted to lie and say it was probably the baby's stinky diaper, but I opened up to her

and revealed that I, in fact, was the stinker. Of course, this whole conversation had to wait until we made it into the van. And, since the smell followed us, I knew it was not the fault of the big, sweaty man in front of us in line.

There were many times that day I had thought about taking a shower, and then something would happen. Leah always seemed to be hurting herself or Lainey, and just didn't quite grasp the fact that babies were not easily glued back together. So, I was always on the run helping Lainey dodge plastic baby doll heads or hard rattles clocking her upside the head. And, I knew there was something I kept meaning to do but could not for the life of me remember what it was until my dear Leah reminded me. The humid Virginia summers do not mix well with two-day-old sweat and leaking breast milk.

Reason #2

You keep searching for the "perfect opportunity." The most common reason for not showering or bathing is usually because you keep waiting for the opportune time to do so. This time, you will find, or already have found, may never come. So, you just have to do it, ladies! Just jump in and cleanse those pores, exfoliate that skin, and wash away your odor. Your family and friends will thank you for your tubby time-outs.

Of course I would not lead you into the shower or bath without advising you on how to actually enjoy such a luxury in colic land. As with chocolate time-outs, an escape to a relaxing bath or shower is crucial to your peace of mind. Without these breaks from the cries, you may find yourself going completely mad. I did. And, that is why I now know that you must mandate and demand these moments alone, however brief and short-lived they may be.

Whether you are in the mood for a quick, refreshing shower or a long, relaxing bubble bath, see the box below for some tips to make your experience an enjoyable one.

BATH AND SHOWER TIPS

Tip 1: Make sure baby is recently fed, burped, diapered, and loved

Tip 2: If you don't have a husband or helper on hand, bring her to a safe room and put her in a safe place, such as a playpen

Tip 3: Walk away

Tip 4: Turn the baby monitor off

Tip 5: Turn the bathroom fan on

Tip 6: Put on some relaxing music

Tip 7: Go to your happy place

Tip 8: Enjoy

THE PERFECT BATH PRESCRIPTION

The perfect bath involves taking full advantage of all five senses.

Smell

There are many, many aromatherapy products, and these fragrances can help improve mood and enhance relaxation. For a perfect aromatherapy bath, add ten drops of one of the following scented oils into warm water, depending on your mood, and soak for fifteen minutes:

• Feeling stressed out? Try some lavender, chamomile, or sandalwood

- Are you sad? Jasmine, neroli, or lavender may help
- Mad? Reach for some chamomile, lavender, or neroli
- Mentally exhausted? Pour in some lavender, peppermint, or rosemary

Yes, it appears that if you are feeling any and/or all of the above, lavender is the perfect oil for you!

Obviously, if you develop a rash from any of these oils, don't use them again.

Touch

Running your hands back and forth through warm, silky water is a relaxing experience. The heat instantly soothes, comforts, and cleanses your pores.

Sight

Dim the lights, and get in the mood. Light some candles, kick back, and watch shadows dance on the walls.

Sound

Play some relaxing melodies to help you escape. Frank Sinatra is one of my favorites and so is classical. Other soothing sounds include those of nature, such as rain or the sound of waves tumbling on shore. But I would avoid the sounds of tropical rain forests. My sound machine offers that option, and it makes me feel like I'm locked in a cage with a giant toucan on crack—not my idea of a good time.

Taste

You know what I am going to offer up here—something chocolate, of course, or even a glass of wine, or beer, if you so desire. For the wine drinkers, try some chardonnay with grapes, cheese, or strawberries dipped in chocolate (if by chance someone brings these over—I know you don't have much time for fondues these days). If you are a beer girl, then go for an amber, if you want to add chocolate. And, for those who choose not to partake in adult beverages, go for a Shirley Temple and some chocolate-covered cherries. Of course, as with everything in life, moderation is key. You're already tired enough and alcohol is a depressant. But one glass of wine or a twelve-ounce beer should be just fine. And if you're breast-feeding, you can pump the alcohol out later.

. . .

You are now perfectly set up for a relaxing water getaway. So, what are you waiting for? Secure the baby, gather up your belongings, and head to the bathroom for some well-deserved rest and relaxation.

Cheers!

10

Where's the Floor?

AS YOU WELL KNOW, YOUR PERSONAL HYGIENE IS NOT THE only thing that suffers in the land of colic. Your house takes a beating, too. But, don't worry. Just follow some trusted advice from the late and great Erma Bombeck, and your home should make it through just fine:

> *My theory on housework is, if the item doesn't multiply, smell, catch fire, or block the refrigerator door, let it be. No one else cares. Why should you?*

Great advice, don't you think?

For me, the floors took the brunt of the filth. When I was pregnant, I just gave up bending over, and you could follow my binge trail to a T. My husband would often come home and say things like, "I see someone got into the pretzels today," or "Wow, someone sure was hungry. It looks like they started with sesame seed bagels, then went for the chips, and ended with ice cream and chocolate syrup."

Yes, it is true that I often left a mess behind. And, I give my husband credit for referring to me in the third person. If he had tagged me specifically as the food-dropper-leaver, I would have probably been a little upset. After I delivered Lainey via C-section, I became even more of a slob, but at that point I could have cared less.

I know there are some people out there who just can't rest if their home is not in complete and total order. Many of my friends are like that. Some are just the opposite, but for those who fall somewhere in the middle you will find that cleaning your house is done on an as-needed basis right now—such as when your house begins walking away on its own or when someone wants to come and visit. As you know, new babies beget visitors and no one wants to be perceived as unsanitary, especially if the person coming by happens to be someone you may want to impress, such as your super-clean Aunt Nancy or, heaven forbid, your husband's boss. I know how hard it can be to gather up your wits at a moment's notice and get your house in order, so what follows are some tips for making your house presentable in a jiffy:

For the Mess

—*Step 1, Quarantine.* Decide which rooms your guest will most likely enter, and restrict their visit to those given areas. Close all the doors to any rooms where visitors need not be. This usually leaves you with the task of having to clean only the family or living area, the kitchen, the baby's room, and, if you have one, the guest bath.

—*Step 2, Rake and Dump.** If you are blessed with a home that has a lot of closets, you are a very lucky woman. One saving grace for me was that I happen to live in an older home equipped with enough closets in which to hide a few families. So, I took full advantage, and when visitors were coming, I'd rake the floors, tables, and bathroom counters clean, and then empty the contents into the closets. Most of the refuse consisted of toys, dirty laundry, and some spit-up towels. You can also utilize the space beneath the bed or under the crib.

*WARNING: For the kitchen, I don't recommend the rake and dump method. This is one room where you have to decide what is important. If you have enough time to get rid of the dirty dishes or throw them in the dishwasher, then wonderful. If not, just rinse them off and throw them in the sink along with some soap. This will at least make it look as though you were starting to wash them.

—*Step 3, Wipe.* Grab some paper towels and glass cleaner or all-purpose cleaner, and go crazy. Or don't. It depends on the guest. If you're going to be serving some sort of snack, such as chips and dip, it's probably best to wipe that area of the serving table clean of any debris or sticky stuff.

For the Smell

Chances are, your house smells a little raunchy right now. Diaper disposal systems can only hide so much, in spite of their claims. Luckily, there are plenty of products designed to help mothers in need. My favorites are the plug-in air fresheners—vanilla and fresh linen, specifically—that last for a good week or two. Other things to try include the spray-on carpet foam that you don't have to vacuum up (FYI: Make sure the carpet is dry before placing your infant directly on it) and, of course, sanitizing room sprays come in a variety of pleasing aromas.

Scented candles are another favorite, but please use caution. Right now, it's probably hard enough for you to remember to feed yourself; just make sure you don't forget to blow out the candles. And, if you want to get fancy, try simmering some potpourri on the stove. My favorite is apples and cinnamon, especially during the winter months. Of course, it also requires that you remember to turn off the burner after your guests depart.

For the Lack of Embarrassment

There will be times you just don't get the chance to clean prior to the arrival of company. In these situations, at least make your guests wait at the door while you quickly hide all the embarrassing items that are probably lying around. First off, check the guest bathroom for garbage pails overflowing with sanitary napkins and/or dirty underwear or bras. From there, make your way to the living area for any breast shields sitting on tables. And don't forget to put on a bra and gargle with some mouthwash!

Just so you know, I am in no way, shape, or form a domestic goddess. It is highly unlikely that Martha Stewart would ever approach me with an offer to take over her business, and I am okay with that. I do, however, feel I represent the average mother, and although I do like to keep my house presentable and livable for my family, I am not out to win any awards for doing so.

As for the courageous souls who like to do the "drop-by's," to heck with them. I would never, ever just drop by a new mother's house unless she made it crystal clear that it was okay to do so. Even then, I would probably still not do it. It's just plain rude, if you ask me. Odds are, if the doorbell rings, you have either just laid the baby down or just started nursing her. And, if by some chance you weren't doing either, then you were probably still in your pajamas, braless, and have not yet brushed your teeth. As for the appearance of your house, it is most likely in complete disarray. It's okay. They will get what's coming to them when they're greeted at the door by a set of giant, leaky boobs and a screaming baby flopping about. They may just actually be so scared that they never do the drop-by again.

SECTION THREE
Belly Rubs, Show Tunes, and Vacuums
What to Do When the Noise Starts

Mothers are born with an instinctual sense of what to check for when their baby cries. With the first whimper, we begin the process of trying to figure out what it is our baby needs. We offer our breast or a bottle, in case they are hungry. When that fails, we place them over our shoulder and try to burp the cries away. Then we peek inside their diapers to see if a fresh one is needed and check the temperature of their hands and feet to make sure they aren't too hot or cold. All the while, we cradle them in our arms and stroke their sweet heads to try and console them. If all of the basic checks are complete, and baby has a clean bill of health, that is when the real games begin.

Although there is no magic bullet for colic and crying, the following chapters provide an array of time-tested techniques that may be of help. You will learn the art of juggling back and forth between methods to learn which one works best at that given moment. As you will, or already know, what works one day may not work the next. But the good news is with each day that passes, you are that much closer to the end of your colicky days.

11

Buyer Beware

I WAS, AND AM STILL, AMAZED BY THE WIDE ARRAY OF PROD-
ucts available online that are touted to cure colic. The fact
is, if there was a cure for colic and fussy infants, we would
have already heard about it! It would be on the front page
of every newspaper and parenting magazine in existence.
So, I am sad to say that, as of yet, such a cure does not actually exist.

In your desperation, you are likely to start surfing the
net for possible solutions. But, just so you know, most of
these "colic cures" are a big waste of money. I confess, I
was taken by one of these products myself. It was supposed to be a "magical" CD with "scientifically proven"
calming melodies. All this ten-dollar CD did was make me
realize how tired I actually was. As for Lainey, she still
screamed bloody murder.

"Gripe water," which is a liquid blend of various herbal
products, is one of the most marketed online products for
colic, and it may, in fact, be dangerous. Considered a "food

supplement," it's not required to meet the same strict reg-
ulations and standards as prescription drugs. And, most
alarmingly, the manufacturer does not have to prove the
product to be either safe or effective. It's only after a product has been exposed as harmful or dangerous that it is
taken off the market.

Case in point: Recently, one of the most popular, over-
the-counter gripe water products was recalled due to
contamination. After a six-week-old infant became ill
with diarrhea, the Food and Drug Administration (FDA)
found the gripe water used was infected with a parasite
called cryptosporidium. This parasite can cause severe
disease in young children and immunocompromised individuals. That's why you need to be so cautious when it
comes to ordering "cures" online, without a doctor's okay.
You never know what you're going to get, and who wants
to take any chances with their little one?

Also, despite what your Great Grandma Betty may
have told you, always check with your baby's pediatrician
before giving her any sort of folk remedy for colic. Some
remedies are relatively harmless, whereas others may
pose a serious risk to your baby. For instance, some cultures believe that illness is caused by impurities, and
these impurities need to be eliminated from the body
through the use of laxatives (i.e., castor oil and senna) or
diuretics such as teas. Giving a young infant a laxative
or herbal tea concoction to help her eliminate her "impurities" can quickly lead to dehydration and even death.
Other folklore remedies mentioned in the literature included asafetida, bicarbonate, and paregoric. The use of
asafetida, which is often sold as a tincture or powdered
spice, has been associated with a rare blood disorder

that affects the body's ability to transport oxygen. Bicarbonate can cause dangerously high sodium levels, and paregoric, which is derived from opium, can lead to respiratory depression.

EAR PROTECTION ADVISORY

Living with a colicky baby can cause damage to your ears. The average shrill of a newborn measures at about 84 decibels, which equals the sound pressure generated by a passing freight train. According to scientists, anything that's 85 decibels and higher can cause permanent damage to your inner ears, and this is why you need to know how to protect your ears and the ears of your loved ones.

The basic earplug offers affordable and quick protection in times of colic fits, but the protection is minimal. While earplugs help dampen the sharpness of the cries, you can still hear them loud and clear. But there is good news. The world of electronics has come up with an amazing invention: noise-canceling headphones. You can still hear the cries, but the intensity at which you hear them is greatly reduced, making your nerves and your eardrums less rattled. There are many different models available, and some are more expensive than others, ranging in price from $35 to upwards of $300. Most of them get the job done, however, which is decreasing the shrill of your baby's cries. Of course, you should test them out first, and make sure that you can, in fact, still hear your baby if she does cry. For the youngsters of the household, I recommend buying a regular set of kid-sized headphones since most of the noise-reducing headphones are made for adults.

So, in times of a colic crisis, don yourself and your family

continued

members with some headphones so that you can make sure your ears are working properly when your baby says her first word–and I hope it's a resounding, "Mommy!"

I have also heard of some very strange, yet relatively harmless "cures." For instance, one mother told me her grandmother put onions in the baby's socks to get rid of colic. She swore that it worked. Another mother told me about the "healing powers" of African cowry shell bracelets, but I would strongly caution against their use since they pose a potential choking hazard.

Bottom-line: Always consult your baby's pediatrician before giving her anything or trying any strange folk remedy that you may have heard of. The risks are just too great.

There are, luckily, many safe techniques that can help calm colicky and fussy infants some of the time. And most of these methods do not require forking out any money whatsoever. If there are any products that I think are truly must-haves in colic land, I will point them out in the following chapters. Otherwise, take advantage of the many colic soothers that can be found right inside your home or out on your back porch.

12

The Diet Dilemma

YOUR BABY HAS JUST EATEN. HER DIAPER IS DRY, AND SHE IS warm and cozy and lying in your arms. But she is screaming bloody murder! What could possibly be wrong? After you have completed all of the necessary checks and consulted with your baby's pediatrician, it's a good idea to look at your baby's diet. I know, all she drinks is milk. She's not eating Big Macs and French fries, yet, but there is a chance that what your baby is eating may be contributing to her frequent fussiness.

Whether your baby is breast-fed or bottle-fed, he is equally likely to suffer from colic.

As a breast-feeding mother, I tried really hard to keep track of what I ate in order to see if I could find any correlation between what I consumed and Lainey's outbursts. Of course, I never did find any particular food product that seemed to be responsible for all our misery. So, I just kept on eating what I normally did and kept on listening to Lainey's wails. Studies have found, however, that a one-week trial of a low-allergen diet may help decrease the amount of time colicky infants cry. I was not willing to attempt this, but you may be and it might very well help:

For the breast-feeding moms, you can try eliminating certain well-known food allergens from your diet for one week and see how your baby responds. Foods to avoid include: cow's milk, eggs, peanuts, tree nuts (i.e., almonds, walnuts, macadamia nuts, cashews, hazelnuts, pecan, and pine nuts), wheat, soy, and fish. Now, this is very hard to do since so many products are made from these ingredients. But, if you are desperate for relief, it wouldn't hurt to try it for seven days. And there are products out there dedicated to meeting the needs of people who are allergic to these same ingredients. For example, rice is one of the most non-allergenic foods, and its rewards have been capitalized on in the production of a variety of dairy-free food products. For example, I love ice cream and really don't like to have to go without. Thankfully, an ice cream called Rice Dream Ice Cream® is available in a variety of flavors and is free of dairy and wheat. There is also rice milk that you can use on your cereals and in baking. Just conduct an Internet search for "low-allergen diets," and you will be directed to a multitude of Web sites stocked with recipes and links to assist you with your allergen-free diet if you, in fact, decide to try it. If not, don't worry about it!

Here are some other important notes for breast-feeding moms:

—*Limit your caffeine.* Generally speaking, it's a good idea to limit caffeinated products to a minimum since high levels of caffeine can contribute to irritability in infants. The key is moderation. It's fine to have one cup of coffee, but a whole pot of fully loaded java is likely to send your baby over the edge. Besides coffee, other commonly consumed caffeinated products include tea, sodas, and chocolate. Also be aware of the latest and greatest fad: energy drinks. Most of these so-called health drinks are laced with extraordinary amounts of caffeine. Even Crystal Light, a sugar-free drink, is available in a caffeinated form—Crystal Light Energy—so be careful. Always check the ingredient list before you buy anything.

—*Avoid any un-prescribed over-the-counter drugs or herbal products.* This also includes energy drinks, which are often enhanced with herbs and vitamins, some of which may not be appropriate for a breast-feeding mother. Always check with a lactation specialist before taking any new prescription or over-the-counter remedies.

—*Eat what you enjoy.* Contrary to popular belief, there is no clear evidence that spicy or acidic foods adversely affect your infant. Depending on where you live, your infant may be hooked on jalapeño poppers or wasabi. Other infants may detest them, but it purely depends on each individual. And just because a particular food—such as broccoli—may cause gas in the mother does not mean it will cause gas in the baby. This is because breast milk is made from what passes into the mother's blood, not what's in her digestive tract. So all of the gassy chemicals are filtered out by the time they reach baby.

—*Stay hydrated.* Remember to drink lots and lots of water. Breast-feeding takes a lot out of you—literally!

You can always try keeping a food diary in your spare time (hee, hee). But chances are, by the time you think you have the culprit nailed down, your baby's colic days will be long gone.

For the formula-fed babies, I have good news and bad news. The good news is moms don't have to worry about limiting what types of foods they eat. The bad news is they have to pay for it. Formula is not cheap. I highly recommend buying it in bulk when possible. And after consulting with your baby's pediatrician, he or she will likely suggest a one-week trial of a hypoallergenic formula such as Nutramigen Lipil ®. The most commonly used products for colicky babies are whey or casein hydrolysate formulas. Experts advise beginning with a whey formula first, since they taste better and cost less.

Whether or not Lainey was sensitive to certain foods I will never know. She eats everything under the sun now, with no issues. But if I could go back in time, heaven forbid, I would most likely try a low-allergen diet for a week. Now that I know how easy it is to get your hands on products that are allergen free, I think it deserves a try. Unless, of course, your low-allergen diet makes you more irritable than you already are. If this happens, by all means, don't do it!

Yes, a trial of a hypoallergenic formula may just help decrease the amount of time your baby spends crying every day. Or, it may not. Either way, don't dismay. The next chapters are devoted to a more hands-on approach to soothing your fussy infant and calming your frazzled nerves.

13

The Sucker

THERE IS MANY A MOTHER WHO WORRIES THAT IF SHE OFFERS her baby a pacifier, he or she will never give it up. Now, let me ask you, have you ever seen a grown man with a pacifier dangling out of his mouth? Have you ever walked in on your husband and found him with a pile of pacies? I didn't think so.

The fact is, sucking is a very soothing reflex that infants are born with. Both of my girls sucked their thumbs in utero, as evidenced by ultrasound technology. So it makes sense that offering them a pacie to suck on would help comfort them in times of stress. The problem comes when other mothers judge you when they see your baby "plugged up" with a pacifier. I'll never forget the time I was shopping at a popular baby super store when I happened in on a conversation between a "super mom" and her friend. As they walked down the pacifier aisle, the super mom ranted about how lazy it is to offer your baby a pacifier and how moms should be able to calm their babies using real, hands-on techniques instead. She obviously never had a baby with colic, and I actually did not even see a baby with her, so either she never had one or her baby was one of those freak babies who came out sleeping for eight-hour stretches and never cried. But for the real moms out there, it is in everyone's best interest to at least offer your infant a pacifier if they are in one of their inconsolable crying fits.

There are pros and cons of using a pacifier, of course. I will lay them out for you so you can decide what is best for your baby.

PACIFIER PROS
Decreased Incidence of SIDS

The latest research shows that pacifier use can decrease the risk of SIDS (Sudden Infant Death Syndrome) by 61 percent. Although the reason for these findings still remains unclear, it is speculated that sucking helps infants maintain a heightened sense of alertness and arousal, making them more likely to wake up when their environment becomes unsafe. I am betting that thumb suckers would obtain the same benefit, but that still needs to be investigated.

Satisfies the Sucking Reflex

Infants are born with the need to suck. After all, it is a survival mechanism. They have to learn how to suck in order to get the milk they need out of a bottle or breast. And some babies just aren't coordinated enough to find their thumbs at birth, so offering them a pacifier is usually a welcomed event.

You Can Take Them Away

Unlike thumbs, pacifiers are disposable. If your baby becomes very dependent on their pacifier, that is okay. Just make sure you stock up on the kind she likes. Most children will outgrow their need for them by the time they are two or three years old. A good way to help wean them is to allow them their pacifiers only at nap time and bedtime after they reach a certain age. I actually had a really hard time getting Leah, my first-born, to give hers up, but we did it with great success. We told her that Santa Claus needed all her pacifiers to give to the little babies in the world whose parents could not afford them. She searched high and low for every pacifier in the house and ended up stuffing her stocking with about ten of them. Remarkably, she never asked for one again and was proud of herself for helping out other babies in need. So, where there is a will, there is a way!

PACIFIER CONS
Increased Incidence of Dental Problems

Generally speaking, the use of a pacifier for the first year or so of your child's life does not normally cause any permanent changes in dental health and teeth alignment. It is when children are allowed to use a pacifier after the age of three or four that they are more likely to experience problems with overbites and cavities from continual pacifier use.

May Interfere with Breast-feeding

I have a hard time with this speculation, and that is because Leah was offered a pacifier at birth and had one in her mouth until she was three. She also took to breast-feeding wonderfully. Many experts believe, however, that introducing a pacifier before breast-feeding is well established may interfere with proper latching on. Chances are, if baby has latched on successfully in the hospital and is breast-feeding on a regular schedule by the time you go home, a pacifier won't cause any issues. If your baby is having trouble latching on or is breast-feeding irregularly, you should wait to offer the pacifier during the day until baby is at least two weeks old. This will probably work out well since colic does not normally set in until the same time.

Baby May Awaken at Night When Pacifier Is Lost

This happened to me a lot. Leah would always wake up if she couldn't find her pacifier in the middle of the night, and it was a real pain in the neck having to wake up to get it for her. But I later discovered that once she was old enough to scoot around in her crib, all I had to do was sprinkle her crib with pacies and she would find one on her own.

Greater Chance of Ear Infections

Leah did have more ear infections than my thumb sucker. But Leah used her pacifier all the time. Studies have shown that after your baby reaches six months old, if you try to decrease daytime use of a pacifier, her chances of getting an ear infection decrease substantially.

When you weigh the pros against the cons, the benefits of offering your baby a pacifier outweigh the risks. The decreased incidence of SIDS alone is reason enough to offer your baby a pacifier, at least when he is sleeping. And if you follow some general guidelines, which I've listed below, there are very few negatives involved with pacifier use in babies.

PACIFIER DOS

1. Offer your baby a pacifier when sleeping. After they are six months old, try to discourage daytime use in order to minimize middle ear infections and dental problems.

2. If your infant keeps waking up in the middle of the night for a pacifier, you can use one of the newer pacifier clips on the market that clip onto their clothes. The key here is that the straps need to be very short. If they are too long, there is the risk of strangulation.

3. Keep baby's pacifiers clean. Try to wash them on a frequent basis with warm soap and water. Boil them prior to their first use.

4. Throw away old and/or deteriorating pacifiers. If they look old, trash them.

5. Stock up on baby's favorites. Once you find the kind of pacifier your baby likes, keep your supply stocked. And don't forget to keep extra ones in the crib. My favorite kinds were the ones with glow-in-the-dark bases. Leah was able to find those easier during the middle of the night.

PACIFIER DON'TS

1. Never tie a string around the pacifier. This could pose a strangulation risk to baby.

2. Do not try to make your own pacifiers or use hand-me-downs. Only store-bought pacifiers should be used, and even these need to be parent-tested. Pull on the nipple and make sure it is properly fastened to the base. Never use pacifiers that look old, and

don't use any two-piece pacifiers since they can break and become choking hazards.

3. Don't offer the pacie until breast-feeding is well established. You want to make sure that mommy's nipples are their favorite!

As far as which type of pacifier to buy, it is up to you. Pretty much all the ones on sale in stores today are safe and appropriate. I do recommend buying a few different kinds in the beginning and letting baby choose which one he likes best.

Just so you know, not all babies will want a pacifier, and this is fine, too. If you're worried about SIDS, then try to have them take a pacifier when they are sleeping. Here are some other important SIDS reminders:

- Always lay babies down to sleep on their backs.
- Do not put pillows or blankets in baby's bed.
- Use a firm mattress, and make sure the sheet fits snugly and securely.
- Keep baby's room on the cooler side—extreme heat can contribute to the risk of SIDS.
- Sleeping in the same room as baby, but not the same bed, may decrease the risk of SIDS.
- Never allow anyone to smoke inside your home or around your baby.

. . .

The great pacifier debate is likely to continue, but with the latest findings on the decreased incidence of SIDS, it is likely to come to a halt in the near future. Whether your baby chooses a pacifier, his thumb, or your finger, only you and your baby know what's best.

14

The Swaddle

THE ANCIENT ART OF SWADDLING HAS BEEN USED BY MANY new mothers to help fussy babies calm down. A good, tight wrap has been known to instantly calm both infant and mother alike. There are many reasons to swaddle your baby, such as the following:

- They may just stop crying! That's right, some babies will instantly stop their wailing once they are transformed into baby burritos. Swaddling mimics the tight, confined environment of the uterus and helps them feel safe, secure, and cozy.
- Prevents the startle reflex. This is also called the Moro reflex, and it is that thing you observe when you are watching your baby fall asleep and then, all of sudden, they jump and flail out their little arms. I used to feel so bad for my girls when this would happen. It would seem that right when they were about to drift off to baby dreamland, they would almost jump

out of their skin. This is a normal reflex for infants, and the lack of it may actually indicate a problem. However, since this reflex does startle them so much, a properly swaddled baby will not as likely awaken since their arms and legs are contained.

- Helps infants sleep better. Because swaddling inhibits the startle reflex, it helps them sleep better. Studies have found that infants who are swaddled and laid on their backs to sleep slept longer and had less spontaneous awakenings than non-swaddled infants.

- May decrease the risk of SIDS. A properly swaddled baby may also have a lower incidence of SIDS than a non-swaddled baby. There are two possible explanations for this debatable benefit. First of all, despite the fact that swaddling decreases spontaneous awakenings during non-rapid eye movement sleep (non-REM), it was found to increase awakenings during the REM stage. Are you confused yet? I was. Basically, what you need to know is that swaddled infants do, overall, sleep better and longer. But swaddled infants are also more likely to awaken in response to unfavorable conditions, which is a good thing since it has been speculated that SIDS may be associated with an infant's decreased arousability. Also, the restricted swaddle helps keep infants on their backs, which has also been shown to decrease the incidence of SIDS.

Before you begin to take advantage of the many benefits offered by swaddling, it is important to first know of the proper precautions:

- Avoid overheating. First and foremost, never cover your baby's head. Leave the head completely open. The reason this is so important is that SIDS has been linked to extreme heat. One of the primary ways our bodies release heat is through our heads. If a baby's head is covered, the heat becomes trapped, making the body temperature rise. It is also important to keep your baby's room a little on the cooler side during the hot, humid months. The optimal temperature range is between 70 to 75 degrees Fahrenheit. If your air-conditioner breaks in the middle of the steamy summer, get some fans going to help keep baby's room cool. Infants overheat very fast. Also, pick the right type of swaddling material. The type of cloth depends on how your baby is dressed and the temperature of your home. Common sense rules here. If you are hot, your baby probably is, too. They generally require only one extra layer of clothes, and that consists of a paper-thin onesie. So, if you keep your house between, say, 70 and 75 degrees F, and your baby is in her pajamas, the best type of swaddle to use is a thin one. If you are an Eskimo living in an igloo, then you may want to wrap up baby in something a little warmer!
- Don't swaddle older infants. In general, most infants should not be swaddled during the day after one or two months of age since this restricts their motor development. Once your baby is capable of kicking out of the swaddle, the swaddling days have passed.

So, what is the best way to swaddle your infant? In order to achieve the benefits listed above, you need to find the right swaddling material and learn how to perfect a "tight" swaddle.

I believe the best swaddling blanket around is your baby's hospital blanket. They are the perfect size and thickness. Most of the baby blankets I had at home were more rectangular shaped and not big enough to keep Lainey's arms from escaping. The best swaddling blankets are thin, square, breathable, and big enough for all of your baby's body parts to fit in. A simple at-home trick is to grab a sheet and cut it into equally sized square halves or quarters about three feet wide by three feet long.

Once you have found the blanket, lay it out on the floor and fold the top right corner down about six inches or so. Place baby on her back with her head on top of the fold. Pull the left corner over baby's left arm and tuck it under the right side of right her arm toward her back. Next, pull up the bottom corner over her feet and tuck under the chin. Then pull the right side firmly across toward the left side of baby and do the final tuck under baby's left arm. Now your baby is a little ball of joy!

Quick tip: The absolute best people to ask for swaddling instructions are the baby nurses in the hospital. Before you ever leave the hospital, get these ladies and gents to show you how it is done. They are amazing!

If you don't mind forking out the dough, there are dozens of swaddling blankets available online. My philosophy is, if you can just use one of the blankets given to you as a shower gift, or, better yet, the one from the hospital, keep using those. Or start cutting up some sheets.

After that, if you still don't think you are swaddling your baby correctly, then it may be time to search for an easier alternative. Most of the swaddle blankets are really easy to use and aren't that expensive. Pick whichever one you like best. They all accomplish the same thing—soothing your baby.

I always felt guilty when I swaddled my baby girls. It seemed like I was putting them in a straight jacket, restricting their control over their bodies. But when it comes down it, most new babies prefer the security and coziness offered by a good tight swaddle. You know your baby best. If she screams louder and more violently after being swaddled, then you need to try some other options. Take Lainey, for instance. She hated to be swaddled. So her startle reflex was in full gear during her colic days. I could see her little bassinet bounce every time she would start to fall asleep. But that's how she liked it, I guess.

As for the rest of you, swaddle away.

15

Infant Massage

ONE OF THE GREATEST GIFTS YOU CAN OFFER YOUR BABY, AND yourself, can be found right at your fingertips. Our hands hold the power to touch, love, and bond with our new babies through the art of compassionate touch and infant massage. In this delightful dance, your infant takes the lead as you both fall in love with each other. Not only does infant massage allow you to learn more about your baby's wants and needs, but it also offers emotional, physical, and spiritual benefits for both mother and child.

In order to appreciate the many rewards found in infant massage, you need to start at its roots. It was in a small village in northern India where Vimala McClure, the "mother of baby massage in the United States," witnessed a remarkable event. Lying nearby on a very uncomfortable dirt floor was a mother massaging her tiny infant. The air that surrounded them was not filled with sadness or despair, but it was brimming with happiness and content. The love between this mother and baby was magnificent.

Luckily for us, Vimala sensed the magic of this special moment between mother and child, and captured it. She discovered that the people of this small village seemed to have so little, but, in fact, they had it all. They were nurturers. When a person became ill, they went to them, massaged them, and made that person feel cared for, appreciated, and loved.

And because of the unadulterated love these men and women expressed toward one another, their children followed suit. These kids were not at all aggressive but, instead, were openly loving because of the way they were raised and cared for. Vimala realized how children in America, and society as a whole, could benefit from the traditions of these villagers, and she went on to develop the world's first international infant massage organization. The International Association of Infant Massage (IAIM) is a non-profit family service and education organization headquartered in Sweden with chapters all over the world—including the United States.

It was through my discussions with Suzanne P. Reese, author of *Baby Massage: Soothing Strokes for Healthy Growth*, that I came to understand the amazing roles that infant massage and compassionate touch can play in fostering a loving bond between mother and child. Suzanne is also a Certified International Infant Massage Educator and Trainer with Infant Massage USA, the non-profit U.S. chapter to the International Association founded by Vimala McClure. Suzanne explained the history, benefits, and techniques of infant massage so that I may pass them on to you.

BENEFITS OF INFANT MASSAGE
Relaxation and Relief

Sleep is probably at the top of your list right now. Studies show that infants who are regularly massaged, assuming the touch is nurturing and compassionate, sleep better. It makes sense. When we are massaged, we sleep better, right? This is because massage signals the body to release melatonin, a chemical that helps regulate our sleep/wake cycles. Massage also causes our bodies to release oxytocin, our body's "love" hormone, which helps us experience pleasure, decreases pain, and reduces stress and anxiety. As a result of feeling happy and content, babies sleep longer and sounder. It's a win-win situation!

Stimulation

Depending on your technique, massage can also be stimulating. Downward strokes are most often used to relax, whereas upward strokes are stimulating. Now, it is important to note that massage stimulates both the mind *and* the body. Mentally, infant massage is stimulating because it evokes a sense of parental empowerment—the feeling that you have some control over your baby's well-being. Colicky babies tend to make mothers and fathers feel like complete idiots, whereas infant massage helps them feel as if they are doing something right, for once! Babies also feel empowered and are more able to recognize their own bodies and body parts, such as toes, fingers, legs, and arms. This is, in part, because massage stimulates production of myelin sheaths that wrap around nerve fibers and help babies with development of fine and gross motor skills. So, if you are hoping for a baby Picasso, massage away! There are also techniques specifically for colicky babies that help stimulate digestion and elimination in order to alleviate intestinal discomfort and gas.

Interaction

Our bodies need to be touched. Without human touch and human interaction, babies fail to thrive, and important physical and mental connections never develop. Not only does massage provide an opportunity for parents to connect with their babies, but siblings and other caregivers can participate as well. This improves babies social skills and helps them learn that they are cared for and respected. Also, communication is enhanced by the interactions between you and baby. With time, you learn to recognize verbal and nonverbal cues from your baby, which will help bridge the communication gap between a well-spoken adult and babbling baby.

HOW TO MASSAGE YOUR COLICKY BABY: A STEP-BY-STEP EXAMPLE

Note: Always consult your baby's pediatrician or a certified infant massage educator before attempting to perform massage on your newborn to ensure you are helping and not hurting her.

   —*Step 1. Tell your baby it is time for a massage.* Explain that it is time to do this, so that you can help them feel better. Some parents will start the massage before a colicky fit ensues, while others find that their baby responds better in the midst of it all. It is up to you to recognize what your baby wants. Here are some verbal and nonverbal cues to look for:

"Yes, I want you to massage me."

- Eyes wide open and looking up
- Open arms
- Body relaxed
- May reach out to you and smile

"No, I do not want a massage."

- Closed position: pulls in arms and legs towards body
- Not establishing eye contact
- Crying
- May even push you away

—*Step 2.* Relax yourself and mold your hands over your baby's body.

—*Step 3.* Look at her and tell her you are going to give her a massage so that she feels like she's included in the plan to wellness.

—*Step 4.* Apply some oil. Use a type of oil that you would cook with such as olive oil or safflower oil. Do NOT use baby oil. It is highly flammable and can cause respiratory problems if inhaled. The rule to follow is if it's an oil that is safe to ingest, then it is probably okay to use for infant massage. Make sure you test your baby's response to the oil, first, by applying a small amount on his arm or leg. As long as no reaction is noted (i.e., no rash or redness), then it is okay to proceed.

—*Step 5.* Lay your baby on her back and bare her belly.

—*Step 6.* Show baby your hands. She wants to see what you are using to help alleviate her pain.

—Step 7. Begin the massage: For tummy trouble, apply both palms gently, but firmly, on baby's belly around the belly button and under the rib cage. Begin stroking using a clockwise motion since this mimics the direction of intestinal movement. Then, using your left hand, continue moving around all the hours on the clock. The right hand will follow closely behind.

—Step 8: When you are done massaging, let baby know by telling her, and perform one last cycle.

• • •

There you have it—one of the many techniques taught by the best of the best in the infant massage community. The above example is one of many, and in order to take full advantage of the benefits of infant massage, it's best to consider enrolling in a class.

If you are interested in a class, you can call your local hospital to ask about programs in your area. Many social services departments can also refer you to classes, some of which are free or cost only a minimal amount—or go straight to the source and seek out a Certified Infant Massage Educator at www.infantmassageusa.org. If you've left the mainland for ventures abroad, try finding a local chapter at www.iaim.net. Not only will an infant massage class help you bond with your baby, it will also allow you to meet other parents in the community with the same questions and concerns. No one should be left to battle colic alone.

There are also special techniques that can be performed upon baby waking, baby going to sleep, and routines for any time of the day. It's all about establishing that closeness between you and baby and reassuring each other that you are truly in this together, forever.

I must confess, I never took an infant massage class, but I really wish I had—it would have helped me tremendously. No, massage has not been proven to cure colic. Nothing has. But the sense of parental empowerment and mutual bonding offered through infant massage would have eased many of my pains and frustrations. My self-confidence and self-esteem were in major need of a pick-me-up, and I believe that massaging Lainey could have sent my spirits soaring. In fact, Suzanne has witnessed with her own eyes how mothers and fathers can be transformed from depressed, hopeless parents into joyful, confident caretakers. I wish you and your family the same.

What are you waiting for? Go learn how to massage your baby so that you both feel better! And, while you're at it, get someone to massage you.

16

Babywearing

I COULD KICK MYSELF FOR NOT KNOWING A THING ABOUT slings during Lainey's colic months. I would often see moms toting around their infants in these complicated looking wraps and slings. I would also see these same moms easily breast-feed their quiet and content baby without one little areola exposure. How did they do this? It was all in the sling. There were many moms I met while out and about who raved about baby slings, but by looking at them, I didn't feel at all confident that I could actually figure out how to use one.

I just used my older baby carrier—you know, the kind where you carry baby in front of you, belly to belly or back to belly, depending on their age. Leah loved this thing. Lainey hated it. Really hated it. It was pretty easy to use, but by the time we stepped out the front door, she'd start to wail. With Leah, I could just plop her right into the carrier and vacuum, or eat, or even take a nap. Lainey would have nothing of the sort. But I do believe, after actually having the time to conduct some research, that she would have probably liked a sling.

Slings allow baby to nestle into your body more so than the traditional baby carriers. Whether your baby wants to lie down, sit up, or go for a piggyback ride, slings and wraps offer her the freedom of choice. Traditional baby backpacks, on the other hand, force babies into an upright position, which limits their freedom of movement and can put more stress on their spines.

The intimidation factor is why I never tried a sling. They just looked much too complicated. But I think they can be one of your greatest sanity savers when used appropriately.

BABY SLING BENEFITS

Here is a list of things that will be beneficial to baby in a sling:

—*It can help keep baby calm and content.* Studies have shown that babies who are carried more cry less. Now this doesn't mean you should feel obligated to have baby attached to your hip every second, but you may just find that wearing her around in a sling will actually provide you with more freedom than you expected.

—*Provides closeness with baby.* When you carry your baby close to your body, it provides the warmth and security that babies adore. Especially great is that dad and even big sis or big brother can try it. Dads, in particular, can really use slings to bond with their baby. Unlike yourself, who carried this baby around in you for ten long months, dad never had that experience, so now is the time for him to give it a try!

—*It frees up your arms to do other things.* The most

beneficial aspect of these contraptions, in my opinion, is that they allow you to do other things. By keeping baby snug as a bug in a rug, slings give you the freedom to tend to your other children, clean up around the house, or even take a nap. There are also slings you can buy that you can wear in the pool.

—*Allows baby to see more.* Being little can be hard. Take Leah, my firstborn, for instance. She is very petite, and when you look at the pictures she's taken with my digital camera, you really gain a perspective of the world of a little person. She's always looking up at people who are looking down on her. Slings provide a view of the world that babies are unable to see from the floor where they lie or sit. They get to see what you see, hear what you hear, and smell what you smell.

—*Some babies will breast-feed better.* The position of many slings will place baby in an ideal nursing position. This helps them want to nurse more frequently, which really helps with babies who may not be eating enough or are nursing poorly. What's more, these slings allow for discreet breast-feeding sessions anywhere you go. Whether you're at a restaurant, a park, or at your mother-in-law's, with baby in her sling, you don't have to worry about making anyone around you, or yourself, feel at all uncomfortable. Most people won't even know your baby is nursing!

—*They keep baby safe and secure.* What safer place for your baby to be than wrapped around your waist? Sure, there are plenty of other safe places, but when you're wearing your infant, you know at every second where she is and what she's doing. You never have to run to the other room and check on her. You don't have to keep reminding your other kids that she is not a toy, and you don't have to keep your dog isolated either.

WHICH TYPE TO BUY

There are many different slings on the market, and it can be confusing, not to mention overwhelming, to try to pick the best one for you and baby. Basically, there are three different ways to "wear" your baby:

1. Ring Slings
2. Pouch Slings
3. Wraparounds

The most popular type for beginners is either the ring sling or pouch sling. Slings are usually one-shoulder carriers and can be purchased with or without shoulder padding. There are some distinct differences between the ring and pouch slings. Ring slings are excellent choices for breast-feeding mothers and are easily adjustable to both the size of the wearer and position of baby. They also come with tails that you can use to help cover up while nursing. The pouch slings are good for infants, too, and are easy to get baby in and out of. Their downside, however, is that pouch slings are not as adjustable between babywearers. So, if you want dad to take part in the babywearing process, a ring type is probably your best bet.

The wraps are better suited for the experienced babywearer because of their level of difficulty in getting set up, but this can be learned by a novice with patience and practice. These usually wrap around both shoulders and your waist and offer the best support and comfort for both baby and baby wearer. Parents with back, neck, or shoulder problems would be better off taking the extra time to learn how to use these body-friendly wraps.

You can find slings and wraps in all sorts of fabrics and designs. Organic cotton mesh, smooth cotton, TaylorMade linen, hemp, and Dupioni silk are just a sampling of some of the fabrics. You can also buy very wardrobe-friendly designs—from floral and paisley to stripes and solids—you're sure to find one you like.

WHERE CAN YOU BUY A SLING OR WRAP?

You can purchase a sling or wrap at most of the big baby department stores. There are also a slew of slings and wraps available online in every color and pattern you can imagine. Generally speaking, the most common prices range from $40 to $90. Many of the Web sites also provide instructions on how to use slings. For instance, Sling Station (www.slingstation.com) offers both video and printable instructions online. Some other helpful sites include:

- Baby Flair: www.babyflair.com
- Baby Moon Baby Slings: www.babymoonslings.com
- Mamma's Milk (www.mammasmilk.com)
- Maya Wrap (www.mayawrap.com)
- Rockin' Baby Sling (www.rockinbabysling.com)

If you're truly a babywearing enthusiast, you may want to check out the book *Babywearing* by Dr. Maria Blois. She goes over babywearing in detail and also helps mothers learn how to make their own wraps.

IMPORTANT POINTS TO CONSIDER

—*Make sure your sling or wrap fits correctly.* Most should come with a video and/or instructional pamphlet, but if you buy one on eBay or borrow one from a friend, you may not get the accompanying inserts. If worn inappropriately, you may experience back, neck, or shoulder pain with continued use. In general, it's best to wear your baby higher versus lower and remember to alternate shoulders when wearing slings.

—*Practice wearing your sling or wrap with a baby doll first.* This is a must!

—*You're not spoiling your baby by carrying her around.* It is comforting for babies to be close to their mothers, and it increases their level of security and contentedness. Of course, don't keep baby glued to your hip all the time. She needs to have playtime on the floor and needs to learn how to crawl around and all that good stuff. But while she is in her colicky months, lots of carrying time is a good thing.

—*Avoid wearing baby while performing any hazardous tasks.* For instance, while cooking, mowing the grass, or engaging in any extreme sports, baby should not be on your hip. Grease splatters, sticks fly, and bodies tumble.

—*Remember to look out for any floor hazards.* Carrying your baby decreases your ability to see obstacles in your path, such as toy cars on stairs or spilled milk in the kitchen.

—*Make sure it's secure.* The slings available today are generally made from very strong materials and are made specifically for the purpose of carrying babies. That said, it's always a good idea to check for any recalls at www.cpsc.gov, the Web site for the U.S. Consumer Product Safety Commission. And slings shouldn't show any signs of being less than secure, such as tearing or thinly stretched fabric.

—*Always dress baby according to the weather.* It is extremely important to not let your baby overheat. The slings that are heavily padded are especially prone to making your baby heat up, so dress them appropriately.

. . .

There you have it. You now know more than you ever wanted to know about slings, but they can really help! I see mothers come into the pharmacy with their little kangaroos all the time. Not once have I heard one of these sling babies crying—pretty remarkable.

17

Swaying the Night Away

"Music is the art of the prophets, the only art that can calm the agitations of the soul; it is one of the most magnificent and delightful presents God has given us." —Martin Luther

WHEN BABIES ARE IN THE WOMB, THEY ARE CONSTANTLY ON the move. With every step you take, they jiggle to and fro. Babies become accustomed to this back and forth motion, and many of the best ways to calm fussy babies involve imitating these soothing sways.

MUSIC

I am a lover of all kinds of music. Whether it's the tropical vibes of Jimmy Buffett or the instrumental harmonies of Mozart that send your spirits soaring, take advantage of the gifts of music. Just as with writing, music can do wonders for the soul. Depending on your music selection, it can soothe your nerves, rev you up, or allow you to reminisce about the days gone by.

Whatever type of music you're into, listen to it. And not only do you need to listen, but you should also allow the lyrics to transport you to a more peaceful place. Grab ahold of baby, close your eyes, and practice your dance moves. I can't even begin to count the number of times I turned to music for support in the wee hours of the morning. I would turn on my CD player, hold Lainey close, and dance around the room in circles until I became dizzy. My arms are now stronger because of it. Who says you can't work out with a baby?

The number one lullaby, in my opinion, is "Hush Little Baby." This song not only helps babies fall asleep, but it's great to use during one of their crying fits. It can be your nice way of saying, "Shut the hell up!" I know that sounds horrible, but that's what I was thinking as Lainey bucked and wailed at two o'clock in the morning. Another of my all time favorites is "Edelweiss" from *The Sound of Music*. Every time I sing that song, I'm reminded of the scene where the father sits and gently strums his guitar, revealing his soft and gentler side to his children and his newly found love.

For those of you who feel as if your voice may make your baby cry even louder, know that babies love the sound of their mother's voice, however crackly and off pitch it may be. Take me for instance. Leah has told me on more than one occasion that she loves my voice. Simon, Paula, and Randy, however, the *American Idol* judges, are likely to disagree.

You can also always just put on a CD and let it take over for a little while. Very near and dear to my heart during my colic months was *Frank Sinatra's Greatest Hits* CD. His voice was so soothing—magical, almost—during those midnight cryfests. Even if Lainey would keep on screaming, I at least felt a little calmer when Old Blue Eyes was singing to me.

Music is also a great way to bring you and your baby

closer together as she gets older. There are so many fun children's songs to dance to. I still love "The Bare Necessities" from *The Jungle Book*. As I'm dancing around with my girls, this song helps remind me to stop fretting so much and to relax and realize that life will give us what we need, eventually. I'm sure there are some other songs out there that will give you and your kids equal pleasure and bonding moments.

Whatever music you like, hold baby close and dance around. Of course, be careful with her. She is not old enough for bouncing all over the place just yet. Those times will come soon enough.

WAYS TO MOVE WITH YOUR BABY
Dance Positions

You've heard it from plenty of advice-givers, but this one's really true: There are certain ways colicky babies like to be held. While dancing, many like to be held chest to chest, and they like the skin-to-skin contact as well. Other positions include the neck nuzzle. You can rest baby's head under your neck and let her listen to the vibrations of your voice as you sing. The football hold is another good one. Just put baby belly down on your forearm with her head resting in the crook of your arm while you secure baby with your other arm.

Rockers

When your arms and legs become weak, there are other ways you can keep baby moving without too much effort on your part. One of the most cherished pieces of furniture in my home, still to this day, is a beige glider I bought before Leah was born. So many memories are associated with that chair. Every night, when I tuck in Lainey, now two-years-old, I rock her and sing "Hush Little Baby." It takes a whole two minutes and afterward she is sleepy enough to go down to sleep without a fight. In fact, she actually darts up the stairs ready and eager to go into her crib. Remarkably, as a colicky infant, Lainey hated the glider. And let me tell you, it took a lot more out of me to stand up and dance with her than it did to sit my bottom down in a chair, put my feet up on an ottoman, and glide away. Whenever Leah was upset as a baby, all I had to do was rock her, and she would calm down. I know. You're not supposed to compare your kids. They are all special in their own way and all of that good stuff, but you begin to expect that what works for one baby will work for the next. When it doesn't, it is always so alarming!

Leah was the type of baby who could fall asleep only if rocked. That tradition was carried out until she was about seven months old, and my husband and I decided our "rocking-baby-to-sleep days" were over. It became a fight between Mike and me every night:

"It's your turn to rock her tonight honey," I would sweetly say.

"No it's not, I rocked her last night," my silly husband would remark.

"Oh no, you didn't. I did. I specifically remember."

"Well, even if you did, I worked all day and am totally exhausted."

"And what exactly do you think I did while you were gone? Do my nails look polished? Does my hair look trimmed? And what does my face look like? Bright, beautiful, and rested? I didn't think so, mister. Now, take the baby and rock her, damn it!"

"Okay."

Yes, that was a typical conversation. So, it's probably good that Lainey didn't like or want to be rocked to sleep back then because that would have been one more battle I would have had to undertake.

Swings

When my attempts at rocking Lainey failed to calm or soothe her, I tried a swing. Swings are a lot more sophisticated than they used to be. They play Mozart and Beethoven symphonies and some are equipped with mobiles and lights, as well. I thought for sure Lainey would like this swing thing. Nope. No luck. Sometimes she would be okay in her swing, but the chances of it helping were pretty low. Some babies, on the other hand, are instantly soothed and relaxed by their swings. My good friend's little girl would actually fall asleep in her swing.

You can also try an outdoor porch swing, glider, or hammock. There were many days I would lay outside in the hammock and nurse Lainey to sleep. The combination of the closeness, warmth of the sun, and gentle rocking was the perfect recipe for slumber, and we both took advantage of it.

. . .

So, sing to your baby. Swing with your baby. And hold your baby tight. With any luck, she will soon fall fast asleep in your arms and, most important, stay asleep when you lay her down.

18

Good Vibrations and the White Noise Effect

GOOD VIBRATIONS

MOVING RIGHT ALONG TO THE NEXT ITEM UP FOR BUSINESS: Vibrators. Now don't get too excited. These are different from what you are likely thinking! Pretty much every baby gadget out there now has a vibrate mode. With the flick of a switch, your baby's bassinet, swing, or bouncy seat can turn into a lean, mean, vibrating machine. The feelings and sounds generated from this motion are often just the trick to help Junior calm down.

My old neighbor used to take full advantage of the vibrations offered by her Dodge Caravan. She could be seen driving around the block more than a dozen times every day for approximately five months. This is because the only way she could get her baby to sleep was with a car ride. Luckily for her, the gas prices were a lot cheaper back then. Regardless of the cost, I was willing to try anything, so I attempted the car ride soothing technique, which of course, completely backfired.

Lainey was never madder, louder, or more red-faced than when we went for a car ride. Trying to go anywhere was wretched. And I was forced to drive like a mad woman because I was always in such a hurry to get from point A to point B, and I would sometimes take risks that I now realize I shouldn't have. But the cries! They were so horrible that I always ended up becoming a contortionist while driving. I would awkwardly twist and stretch out my right arm as far as I could to first find the pacifier, and second to find her mouth and shove it in. I learned how to do the face feel—when you carefully finger your baby's face in order to find her mouth without poking out her eyes or crashing. It's a little tricky, but you get really good at it after a while. My efforts were always unsuccessful. Lainey hated her pacifier and would just spit it out, over and over, and I would keep swerving in and out until I'd eventually give up and let out a loud shriek. Then I'd throw up my arms and turn on the radio as loud as I could and just face the fact that she was going to scream for the entire trip. Fun stuff.

As you can imagine, the car was not my method of choice for soothing my colicky baby, but so many moms have had success with this method. So many moms, in fact, have sworn by car trips that a product simulating a car was made. This battery-powered gadget that attaches to your baby's crib has a vibration unit and sound generator that simulates a car going 55 miles per hour. I think it's a little extreme but, hey, who am I to judge? If this product helps you keep your sanity and your baby happy, then that is wonderful. But just so you know, these car ride simulators have not been found to be more effective at soothing colicky infants than any of the other available techniques, and they are quite pricey ($140).

Another time-tested method for soothing a crying baby is the top-of-the-dryer technique. We've all heard the stories of mothers traveling to laundry rooms with a crying baby in tow, in hopes of finding relief. You can either lay baby on a thick blanket draped over the top of the dryer or place their carrier on top. Either way, common sense rules apply: Don't put baby on a dryer that is too hot, and never leave baby unattended.

Next comes vibrating baby equipment. Pretty much all baby gizmos come with a vibrate mode. Here are just a few:

- bassinets
- crib mattresses
- activity mats
- bouncy seats
- swings
- pack 'n plays

Of course, I am going to tell you what vibrating things Lainey liked: none. The vibrate mode did not phase her a wink. Her swing had it, her bouncy seat had it, and so did her bassinet. I never did try the clothes dryer. Maybe that would have offered more luck for both of us!

THE WHITE NOISE EFFECT

What Lainey did really like, however, was white noise—lots of it. The womb is a very busy, noisy place. So, it's no wonder that babies like the security offered by these familiar sounds once they escape the confines of your uterus. Swishes, swooshes, heartbeats, and gurgles. These are the sounds babies like. Luckily, there are plenty of everyday items found in your home that can mimic these soothers.

Running Water

Water is your friend. You need it to stay hydrated, refreshed, and sane. Take, for instance, the time my family and I decided to go for a family trip. Yes, it was during the colicky months, but I was getting cabin fever, so we jolted down the road to an indoor water park for the night. While Leah slid down slides and splashed through wave pools, Lainey just snoozed away. In fact, Lainey turned into such a calm, tranquil baby that I wondered if something was wrong with her. Then, I closed my eyes for a minute, and it dawned on me—I realized that it was the sound of running water, and probably the warmth of the place, that helped my colicky infant turn calm. It was wonderful. And to top it off, Leah got to have a ball in the process. If that place hadn't been so expensive, I think I would have camped out there until Lainey's colic days were over.

You can also take advantage of the wonders of water by offering baby a bath. Baths are soothing and, as with many colic calmers, being surrounded by water helps remind babies of their life in utero. Unlike the comfy and cozy womb, however, I did notice that Lainey's infant tub looked mighty uncomfortable, so I usually put a warm, fluffy towel under her to add a little cushion. I tried one of those big sponge inserts once, but it got cold too fast. Once you get their baths nice and comfy, you can add to their moment of luxury by placing a warm washcloth across their bellies. Lainey loved this.

Despite your best attempts, some babies really hate getting baths. If this happens, you can try a tubbie for two.

The closeness with mommy may help them calm down long enough to realize how relaxing a bath can be.

Vacuums

There are actually CDs you can buy that play vacuum sounds. But why would you waste money on a CD when you can actually clean your floors and quiet your baby at the same time? Maybe this would work best for those of you who have all hardwood floors. Otherwise, I would just take advantage of the opportunity to clean up a little.

Hair Dryers

If I ever needed a few minutes of quiet, I would start drying my already dry hair. Sometimes the only thing in the world that would make Lainey stop crying was for me to turn on my hair dryer. I have very long hair, so when it is actually wet it takes a good fifteen minutes or so to dry completely. I think her favorite part was watching my hair fly around and anticipating the sporadic tickles that would often fly her way.

Fans

Most homes today come with built-in fans. Every time I made an attempt at cooking, I did so with my kitchen fan turned on high. When I took a shower, I turned on the bathroom fan. In Lainey's room, there was a fan; in my room, there was a fan; and I had ceiling fans in almost every other room, as well. I really don't know what I would have done without them. The humming generated by these gadgets really helped Lainey remain calm and cool.

Sound machines

You don't have to go out and buy a sound machine to calm your baby, but it may help if your home is lacking in fans or other white noise gadgets. They are pretty cheap and can provide you peace of mind in a pinch. Most of these will play the sounds of waves, rain, and wind, to name a few.

. . .

Regardless of your efforts, certain babies, believe it or not, just want some peace and quiet. Several studies have found that too much stimulation can actually aggravate colicky infants. When your soothing attempts have failed, put baby in another room that is quiet and safe, and see if she calms down on her own. Make the room as distraction-free as possible. Dim the lights, close the door, and go in another room and pray this works!

19

Change the Scenery

WHAT HAPPENS WHEN YOU ARE STUCK IN A CONFINED SPACE with a baby who cries and cries? You go crazy, and there is a term for this—cabin fever. If you don't attempt to go anywhere and quarantine yourself in your home, you too will go cuckoo.

Escape is necessary. I don't care if your baby cries wherever you go, just go. Put your earplugs in, drive to your destination, and keep your earplugs in place if baby is still screaming. Chances are, however, the change in scenery will evoke a positive reaction. If you're bored, chances are your baby is, too. Even though your husband says you're the prettiest thing ever, your baby may just be sick of staring at you and the same four walls she has seen since birth.

If your baby is premature or has other medical issues, then obviously consult his or her pediatrician before you go for a night on the town with baby. But for most of you, by the time your baby becomes colicky, she is ready to go out—just choose the place wisely. For instance, the younger your baby is, outdoor adventures may be better than indoor ones. But there will be times when you can't do that. Any extreme temperatures should be avoided, such as when the temperature gauge is below zero or when you can fry an egg on the sidewalk. These would be the times you should avoid long strolls in the park and, unfortunately, will be forced to escape to an indoor place. If this is the case, it may be a good time to dress your baby in a hat that says, "Back off" or something to that effect. You don't want strangers coming up and touching your newborn baby, and they always seem to go for their hands, which is the worst possible place to touch. This is when the protective mommy in you must come out and remind strangers to look but don't touch.

Young infants are especially susceptible to bacterial and viral infections since their immune systems are still developing, so use extra precautions. If grandma has a cold, she should not hold, touch, and kiss all over your baby. I know it's hard to tell her this, and you don't want to hurt her feelings, but she really should realize it is in your baby's best interest to not get sick. Being a mom is tough, isn't it?

Where, then, can you go with your fussy, irritable infant? Here are some of my favorite places:

OUTDOORS

I am a lover of the great outdoors. The fresh air, gentle breezes, and sights of nature are invigorating. And if your baby screams, it's not as if the sounds are echoing off the walls. People can always walk on the other side of the trail, or even leave if they wish.

The Neighborhood Park

Break out your jogging stroller and get rolling! Walk the paths, hike the trails, and climb the hills. All will help you exercise and give baby a chance to see birds, trees, and blue skies.

A Zoo

Most kids love animals, and how can you go wrong? They're colorful, fun to watch, and often quite vocal—kind of like your baby. I grew up frequenting the local zoo, and I still have as much fun there as I did when I was a kid. Although young infants aren't likely to appreciate the rainbow of colors on scarlet macaws, they are likely to appreciate the tail-hanging antics of monkeys and the long, spotted necks of leaf-munching giraffes.

Theme Parks

I consider my family very lucky since we live less than thirty minutes away from two wonderful theme parks. One is the indoor water park I mentioned in the previous chapter, and the other is an outdoor amusement park. Let me tell you, Lainey loved the outdoor fun park just as much as the water-producing indoor one. While outside, she got to smell the sweet scents of cotton candy, watch animals dance, hear people sing songs, and observe her big sister fly an airplane. And the park even had nursing stalls in some of the bathrooms. What more could you want?

Niagara Falls

My family and I recently headed up to the falls, and I bet Lainey, or any colicky baby, would have been instantly soothed by the calming sounds of falling water. The white noise offered by the falls, as well as all of the wonderful shops nearby, would have been a great escape for us. So, if you happen to live in the area, Niagara Falls will likely be a relaxing trip for you and baby.

Your Backyard

If you don't happen to live next door to Niagara or near any fun parks, you can always take your baby outside. Whether you stroll her around the neighborhood or hold her in your lap on the front porch and listen to the birds sing, it sure beats the stale indoor air.

INDOORS

There are plenty of things to do indoors, as well. The trick is trying to keep your baby germ-free in the process. If your community is in the middle of a flu outbreak, then focus on the bigger, more open indoor places rather than the confines of, say, a freestanding restaurant. Whatever you chose, try to pick places that are relatively large and easily escapable: big because you don't want to deafen everyone around with baby's cries, and easily escapable for the same reason.

A Friend's House

This is a great starting place for venturing out, especially if you have close friends and family members nearby. They won't be bothered by your baby's wails and may even let you run to the store on your own while they watch the baby.

A Playgroup

If you can enroll in an infant playgroup, now is the time to do it. These classes allow you to meet other moms, and many allow older siblings to come along. Most of them offer fun, interactive lessons that can help your infant develop fine and gross motor skills.

The Mall

If you go to the local mall and look around, chances are you will see lots and lots of moms pushing strollers. With Leah, I went to the mall all the time. It was a lot harder with Lainey since I also had Leah to contend with. But, if you have older kids in school or a child who is not as adventurous as my Leah is, then the mall may be the place for you. In malls you can find all the stuff moms need: food, clothes, and places to nurse. Dressing rooms are a great place to privately nurse your infant, and you can try on clothes in between.

Aquariums

Once again we have water, and this time you also get fish, and a lot of them. Watching fish swim is almost hypnotic. Add to that the dim lighting and sounds of running water and your baby may just fall asleep! I did not visit any aquariums with Lainey, but she loved the fish on display at Wal-Mart. The closest aquarium for us involved a trip through a tunnel, and I was not going to risk that drive. Tunnel traffic is way too unpredictable. But if you have the luxury of living near an aquarium, it may be a great place to go.

Your Local Fast-Food Joint

When you are feeling really tired but also really need to go somewhere, I recommend your closest fast food chain equipped with a children's play area—if you also have older children. Just bring along some hand sanitizer. Most fast-food restaurants also offer less artery-clogging foods nowadays. But if you're really in need of a pick-me-up, you can usually always find some sort of chocolate dessert on the menu.

. . .

Of course, the best escape is often the kind that is kid-free and involves a back massage, a handsome bellboy, and an oversized Jacuzzi. But, for now, take advantage of the fact that there are many places you can go with your baby; you just have to force yourself out the door!

20

The Boob Tube

THERE IS NOTHING MORE CONTROVERSIAL THAN WHETHER or not you should allow your infant/child to watch television. Whether you're asking the opinion of the American Academy of Pediatrics or your next-door neighbor, you're likely to get very different answers. Some experts say that TV use can defer or delay your children's intellectual development. Others say it can help. I won't bore you with the details of these studies; you just don't have the time for that right now. What I *am* going to offer is my expert opinion as a TV watcher, mother, pharmacist, and colic survivor.

My stance is this: A little bit of television is okay for your kids. One afternoon I was having a "worst day ever" day, and I could not get Lainey to stop crying. She was utterly miserable—and so was I. I thought and thought and then remembered a shower gift Lainey had received from her great aunt—it was a *Baby Mozart* video. I popped that bad boy into the VCR and crossed my fingers. And it worked! Lainey stopped crying. She was instantly entranced by the dancing puppets and didn't make one little peep for fifteen whole minutes. I seized the opportunity to take a shower while she and her sister watched the video.

Of course, this tape was not a magical cure for colic. She didn't always have such a positive reaction, but it never made her worse. And what harm can a tape with colorful puppets and classical background music really do? If anything, it offered her some culture and veg-out time, and we all could use a little of that sometimes. The key here is to use these tapes in moderation and follow the instructions offered at the beginning of the tape. If you make sure baby is safe and secure, you may just be able to shower while he or she watches a video. I don't think the puppets will jump out of the TV screen and capture your baby. I also don't know of any one-month-old infants who are capable of climbing out of their infant seats, but I have heard of toddlers or pets causing harm, so it depends on your unique situation.

Even more important than watching TV in moderation is to make sure you engage in plenty of interactive play with your baby. Many of these tapes are designed to be interactive but aren't often used that way—and that is okay sometimes. Play and touch are so important at this age and cannot be emphasized enough. I know your baby is so tiny and may not laugh out loud just yet, but she loves to see you make goofy faces. She loves it when you do the "This little piggy" game with her toes. And what could an infant want more than to sit in your lap and have you read to her? My point is it's okay to turn on a video for a few minutes sometimes. You both need this time to recoup.

The last thing to consider when allowing such a young infant to watch TV is deciding what is appropriate for them to watch:

GOOD CHOICES

1. *Baby Einstein* tapes: Pretty much all of these are great choices when used appropriately. They have tapes and DVDs, featuring lullabies, animals, and of course symphonies by Ludwig van Beethoven.
2. *Sesame Street*: Big Bird and his friends are fun, engaging, and very educational. What more could you ask for?
3. Animal shows: In this case, I am talking about real live animals. You wouldn't want your child watching *Shark Attack*, but he'd probably enjoy an underwater scuba excursion featuring Dory or Nemo fish.
4. Shows about space: The Discovery Channel often features these, and the combination of the calming voice of the narrator along with the dark hue of the scenery offers a very relaxing medium for baby.

I'm sure there are many more choices that you'll come up with. Just make sure you watch the show before your kids do. It wasn't until I had kids that I became truly aware of the violent nature of children's programming. Some of the classics like *Bugs Bunny* and *Tom and Jerry* are horribly violent. They feature shotguns, characters bashing each other in the head, and people smoking. The list goes on and on. Not only that, but they use a lot of words that

I don't want my now five-year-old using, like "stupid" and "idiot."

I do believe TV time should be limited; but in times of crisis it may just be your saving grace.

COLIC NEWS

As you know, there is no cure for colic. But, I hope and pray that one day there will be. Until then, I thought I would share some of the latest research regarding colicky infants and let you in on some fascinating work currently being studied by Dr. Ronald G. Barr, one of the world's leading colic experts.

A recent study published in the journal *Pediatrics* found that the use of a probiotic called *Lactobacillus reuteri* improved colicky symptoms in breast-fed infants (its role in formula-fed infants is still unclear). The researchers chose to conduct the study on only breast-feeding babies since probiotics have been thought to react synergistically with the components found in breast milk. What they found was amazing. By day twenty-eight of treatment, babies who were given the *L reuteri* drops cried, on average, one hour less per day than those given simethicone drops. Oh, the things I could have accomplished in that hour!

Researchers speculate that *L reuteri* may have an anti-inflammatory effect on the intestine and help reduce pain. Regardless, a trial of *L reuteri* may be worth discussing with your baby's pediatrician if you are breast-feeding and have a baby with colic. (Note: Just make sure you always ask a medical doctor before giving your baby any over-the-counter products. Young infants especially are very susceptible to adverse drug reactions and/or contaminants.) Although the

continued

results sound very promising, more studies need to be conducted in both breast- and bottle-fed infants before any definite conclusions can be drawn.

Last, but not least, is an important concept brought to fruition by Dr. Barr, who works closely with the National Center on Shaken Baby Syndrome. He believes that there is a universal pattern of crying in infants that spans across cultures and even into other mammals besides humans. This crying increases right after birth, then decreases, only to bounce back and peak by the time the baby is about six to eight weeks old. He coined the phrase, "The Period of PURPLE Crying," in order to describe his theory on infant crying patterns:

P: Peaks around two months

U: Unpredictable, often happens for no apparent reason

R: Resistant to soothing

P: Pain-like expression on baby's face, even without any source of pain

L: Long bouts, lasting thirty to forty minutes or more

E: Evening crying is common

Dr. Barr believes crying is actually a good sign and indicates that a baby is healthy. He also thinks that babies who are labeled as "colicky" just represent an extreme on a normal crying continuum. In his opinion, there is nothing at all wrong with these babies, they are just crying longer and sometimes louder than their peers. His goal is to educate parents on the "normality" of crying seen in newborns in hopes to decrease the incidence of shaken baby syndrome. If parents are taught to

continued

expect these inconsolable crying bouts in their babies, as op-
posed to feeling like they are doing something wrong, this will
help minimize the stress associated with frequent fussers. He
also points out that, despite the latest and greatest books and
theories on helping babies calm down, there is no magic bullet. Some methods work for some babies some of the time,
but none works all the time or for every baby. His message for
parents is to realize that it is okay to put the baby down in a
safe place and walk away for a few minutes. But he also believes that parents should first make an attempt to soothe their
crying babies through human contact, cuddling, and comforting. Most important, parents and caregivers must know to
never shake a baby.

SECTION FOUR
The Others
How to Handle Everyone Else

More often than not, a new mother has others, in addition to her baby, vying for her love and attention. Many of you may be married with very needy husbands who just don't quite understand what it's like to be you for a day. And some of you will also have other children grabbing at your pant legs, wanting to be held and cuddled just as the new baby is. Or you may have a pet in your home right now that needs attention and trips to the vet. Even if you're a loner with no one around but you and your baby, you will, at some point in time, be approached by the dreaded super mom when you least expect it. I hope these chapters will help you deal with all of your encounters with "The Others."

21

The Husband

*"If the new American father feels bewildered and even de-
feated, let him take comfort from the fact that whatever he
does in any fathering situation has a fifty percent chance of
being right."* —Bill Cosby

IF A STRANGER HAPPENED TO LISTEN IN ON A CONVERSATION
between my husband and me during the colic months,
they would have thought I was the worst wife in the
world. While I was caring for an inconsolable infant,
high-maintenance three-year-old, and twelve-year-old
deaf dog, my husband's needs were *not* a priority for me.
After all, he was an adult who was perfectly capable of
fending for himself.

And he had the pleasure of escaping to work every day
once colic knocked on our door. For ten to twelve hours
almost every day, he had the privilege of adult conversation, eating without a screaming baby in his arms, and
peeing in peace. He was a very lucky man, indeed. He slept
upstairs alone, I slept downstairs with the baby next to
me in her bassinet. He woke up to an alarm clock after
eight hours of sleep. I woke up to a screaming infant
every two hours.

So, during the brief amount of time that he was home,

I needed all of him—110 percent. By the time he came home at the end of the day, my nerves were shot, and I was completely exhausted. And when he came home and said things like, "What a rough day at work today," I would respond with something like, "Oh, you poor thing, let me massage your feet, you ungrateful soul!" Or " You want to see rough, look at these nipples." These comments usually generated the reaction I was going for: speechlessness.

My harsh words did not elicit the end result I was looking for, however. I expected that he would fully understand, by my hateful words, that I was in dire need of some pampering. Some words of sincere appreciation and empathy were desperately deserved. But to my dismay, he just didn't get it. He had no idea how hard I had it and how good he had it. I know he had no idea because he even had the nerve to ask for sex! What was he thinking?

All day long I gave of myself, and by the time my husband got home from work, I was completely drained. I had nothing left to give. And I don't know why, but this made me feel guilty. I wished that I had more energy. I wished that I could just turn on my sex drive and get in the mood at the drop of a hat. But I have this problem—a problem shared by many women, I'm finding out: I am a perfectionist. I have this inner need to please everyone and, no matter how hard I tried, I seemed I pleased no one. Lainey cried all the time, which would lead to Leah's crying and the dog barking and me pulling my hair out. Then, on top of everything, Mike would come home and expect a greeting fit for a king: an open-armed wife and two loving children running to him for hugs and kisses. What he got, instead, was a screaming baby shoved in his face, a three-year-old begging for candy, and a wife, who resembled Medusa, barking commands at him. But I was doing the best I could. I was trying, and I felt guilty for not being flawless.

I just want to tell all of you that your husband will make it through colic just fine, darn-it. Do not feel guilty. Your husband's place in your world right now is akin to the dust bunnies in your house. He will be kicked to the corner for a few months, but he will be found, eventually, and taken care of. And if you happen to have one of those fantasy husbands, who actually do get that it's hard for you and you're completely drained and you need someone to help out, then bless you!

I have found it is best to be up front and forward with demands in colic land. So, here are some tips to help you deal with the man in your life:

- In order to avoid potential conflict regarding the issue of sex, warn him ahead of time that sex will not exist until colic hell is over.
- Tell him that it is highly likely he will witness bizarre and unruly behavior. Make sure he knows not to ever point that fact out but to accept it and move on.
- Be specific when asking for, or demanding, his help.
- Go ahead and plant the seed that a vasectomy may be coming in the near future.
- His laundry will likely disintegrate with time or become accidentally lost forever.
- Remember that all human beings are flawed individuals, and if your husband is a good one, he will love you no matter what.

And to make sure neither of you runs away, I highly suggest you both recite your "Colic Vows" at least once a week:

The Husband:

I, <u>Husband's Name</u>, promise to love you, <u>Your Name</u>, throughout our colic experience. Together, we can make it through this trying time. I will try to bring you up when you're down and will not ask stupid questions like, "Honey, do you mind if I go play golf with the guys today?" If I ever do mention such idiotic requests, I give you permission to hold me accountable for such actions by employing your punishment of choice. Whether such punishment consists of leaving me alone with the baby for a whole day or scrubbing the bathroom floor on my hands and knees, I shall oblige.

Through the good, and the bad, I will be by your side. Even when you turn into the she-devil, I will still love and support you. When your horns sprout, I will make no mention of them. I will still pretend you are the sweet and loving wife whom I once married.

When you need a soothing massage, I will be there for you. When you need a shoulder to cry on, I am yours. When you need a punching bag, I will throw you a pillow.

I will act unselfishly during this time of stress and will never think of asking you for sex. I will wait patiently until you are ready and able. Anything mean or cruel that you say to me will be forgiven and forgotten forever. I promise to love and cherish you for as long as we both shall live.

The Wife:

I, Your Name, promise to love you, Your Husband's Name, today and forever despite what I may say or do during our colic experience. When you're down, I will try to bring you up. But if I have had a really bad day, I just may not be able to.

Through the good and the bad, I will be by your side. You just may not know it. When I get angry, I may say things I don't mean. Please don't hold them over my head. When you need a shoulder to cry on, you can call your mother. When you need a punching bag, you can go to the gym.

I will do my very best to raise our fussy infant without losing my mind. I promise to be there for you when this is all over. Until then, I promise to always love and cherish you, even though I may act like I don't.

If you can get your husband to recite this and/or sign a written copy, you go girl! And make sure you let all the other moms know how you did it!

22

The Other Children

"If evolution really works, how come mothers only have two hands?" —Milton Berle

I ALWAYS WANTED TWO CHILDREN. TWO, I FELT, WAS THE AB-solute perfect number. An only child would most likely be lonely, three means one will be left out sometimes, and four, well, that is just way too many for me. So, it came to my surprise that two children was not the exact equivalent of one plus one. No one ever told me this important truth and, if they had, I probably would not have believed them.

The first day Lainey and I came home from the hospital I realized what I had gotten myself into, and it scared the hell out of me. Fresh out of the hospital, Lainey and I were nestled into a corner Lazy Boy enjoying some one-on-one bonding while my in-laws, husband, and three-year-old were playing in the kitchen. Then, in her typical fashion, I could see Leah out of the corner of my eye gearing up for one of her running jumps right onto my lap. I did not know what to do. I couldn't get up in time to dodge her. I was petrified of her possibly hurting the baby, not to mention my cesarean incision, so I screamed bloody murder for help. Of course everyone came running and I started into hysterics. A brief meltdown ensued afterward because I knew, immediately, that the next couple of months were going to be damned hard. And then, two weeks later, colic set in.

I quickly realized that I was in dire need of an extra lap and a couple of arms. My favorite phrase came to be, "Leah, mommy is not an octopus. I only have two arms, you know."

For all the mothers of three-year-olds out there, you know this didn't do much in the way of increasing her understanding of why she had to wait, sometimes long periods of time, for me to fulfill her requests. In her little mind, she probably wondered why I couldn't perform the same functions as an eight-armed octopus, but with just two arms. I was, after all, a "big" person who was able to pour a glass of milk when the container was all the way full and could reach the top shelf to get a glass to pour it in.

Alas, neither patience nor the understanding of the limited powers of a mother are traits of young children. Neither is sharing their mommy with a new sibling, and who can blame them? After all, for so long Leah had me all to herself. Now, I had a new baby to care for who just so happened to scream all the time. This not only upset Leah, but it upset me as well, if not more. All I wanted was for both of my darling girls to be happy, and both of them seemed downright miserable all the freaking time. What was a mother to do?

Well, unlike my adult husband, who would be okay if neglected for a few months, I would never have thought of neglecting my baby girls. So, I had to come up with some solutions to help Leah cope with this new, and often unpleasant, member of the family:

Tip No. 1: Show Them Some Attention

—Include the older child whenever possible. One of my good friends suggested I let Leah sit with me when I nursed Lainey. I took her advice, and although it was a little tricky at first, Leah eventually found just the right spot to sit if she wanted to be near me and still stay out of Lainey's way. Leah's tiny stature made nursing with two girls in my lap quite doable. And when I started introducing the bottle to Lainey, I let Leah help feed her. They both thought it was cool! Other things your older kids can do include picking out clothes for the baby and fetching diapers.

—Play a game or read a book when the baby naps. I know that you will most likely want a nap as well, but if you can devote just five or ten minutes to your other child for a book or quick game of Candy Land, he will appreciate it and whine less later on!

—Schedule a date. When your husband comes home or other help arrives, try to escape with your other kids for a brief trip, if at all possible. Go for a bike ride, go see a movie, or, even better, visit the local ice cream parlor and share a banana split. Take advantage of the benefits that a mere thirty or forty-five minutes of alone time with your older children deliver. It's a cyclical thing really: If you try to devote a certain amount of time each day to your other kids, then they'll act better, you'll be happier, and you'll want to spend more time with them. Sometimes it is

just not possible to leave the house, but you can at least travel to another room and pretend you're at the beauty salon or in the middle of a wild jungle searching for rare animals like the four-headed python or an eight-winged butterfly.

Tip No. 2: Provide an Escape

The cries of inconsolable infants are just as stressful for siblings as they are for parents. And luckily for your other kids, they can escape when the baby enters one of her crying fits unless, of course, you are in the car. I kept a pair of earplugs for Leah in the van, and it seemed to help. For older kids, I highly suggest they keep some headphones in the family vehicle if your baby hates the car as much as Lainey did. I wouldn't even have thought about attempting a flight during the colic months. We surely would have been booted off the plane and left stranded in a stinky, sweaty airport in the middle of nowhere.

When you're at home, make sure your kids have a designated area for escape. When the weather is nice, they can run outdoors and play, but when it is in the middle of a blizzard or a heat wave, they'll most likely seek refuge in a climate-controlled environment, such as an upstairs bedroom or basement playroom. It can also be helpful to provide them with a radio or loud fan that drowns out the cries.

In a perfect world, you have a dear friend or relative who can whisk your other kids away to a land of peace and never-ending fun. Now would be a good time to schedule play dates with their friends or a weekend trip to Grandma's house. Both you and your child would benefit from their escape. They will be able to enter a home that is a little less chaotic for a little while, and you'll have fewer tiny hands to contend with.

Tip No. 3: Keep Them Active

By now, I am sure your house has more toys than you have room for. Well, now may be a good time to get rid of those dust-collecting toys and replace them with some great stress-relieving equipment like mini trampolines and giant punching bags. Siblings of colicky babies need to be given the opportunity to release some of their pent-up stress they undoubtedly possess. Any form of exercise is a step in the right direction toward feeling better, both mentally and physically. So, go ahead, jump in and take turns jabbing that big, bad punching bag with your older kids. Just please use caution.

Now is also a good time to teach your other children the importance of chores, if you have not done so already. Daily chores help build self-confident and independent children who also, at the same time, learn the value of a dollar. One of my daughter's favorites is using the Swiffer duster. She collects one quarter for every room she dusts. She knows that when she dusts four rooms, she will earn one dollar—enough to buy a toy at the dollar store. Another of her favorites: washing dishes. Granted, she never really accomplished the task at hand but she had fun doing it, and it would often keep her occupied for a good thirty minutes or so. Just make sure you provide young children with plenty of towels and only a small amount of soap, or your kitchen may be transformed into a giant bubble factory by the time they're done.

. . .

Now you're armed with some strategies to help you deal with the other children in your life. Remember that you are not Wonder Woman. You do not have an invisible jet that helps you escape a colic crisis, nor do you have magical wristbands to shield your other children from your baby's cries. As long as you give your other children lots of hugs and kisses and provide them with food, rest, and shelter, they too will survive the colic experience.

23

The Dog or Family Pet

MY FIRST TRUE LOVE WAS NOT YOUR TYPICAL TALL, DARK, and handsome type, but rather hairy and about knee-high. My whole world once revolved around a big, goofy shepherd mix named Princess. I found Princess abandoned at an animal control shelter, just waiting for someone to come and rescue her. Four years later, I met my future husband, Mike—the second love of my life. After we moved in together, Princess was forced to make some adjustments. Instead of sleeping by my side every night, she was booted to the floor, where she slept on her nice fluffy dog bed. My spare time no longer revolved around what Princess and I could do together but on what Mike and I could do in the few hours we had off from work or school. In time, Princess adjusted, following Mike around and snuggling up under his chair at dinnertime, anxiously awaiting gifts.

When I became pregnant with my first child, five years later, I was convinced that Princess would immediately take to the baby and welcome her with paws wide open. After all, she had adjusted to Mike pretty well. What more could a dog want than a third master?

I had grand illusions about the relationship I imagined my dog and new child would forge. I envisioned my nine-year-old dog instantly morphing into a modern-day, slightly older version of Lassie, or Lady from *Lady and the Tramp*. If the baby fell, Princess would be right there by her side to help her up. When a stranger approached, Princess would stand tall, shielding the baby from the clutches of this unknown person. And, when Leah, my firstborn, started school I imagined Princess following her to and from the bus, scaring the heck out of anyone who dared to pick on her.

To ensure Princess lived up to my expectations, I logged onto the Internet and searched for the best ways to introduce a pet to a new baby. I read articles, glanced through books, and felt confident that I had adequately prepared Princess for the baby's arrival.

Princess did not exactly take on the role that I had hoped for. Dogs, and pets in general, have an inborn sense of familial hierarchy. When your pet is the first to occupy the home, he considers himself third in the pecking order, after you and your significant other. When you introduce a brand new baby into the mix, though, most dogs feel horribly displaced, viewing the baby as a brother or sister who receives a whole lot more attention then he ever did. And a colicky baby, well, as you can imagine, can lead to a good old-fashioned case of sibling rivalry.

After Leah arrived, Princess began acting more like a jealous boyfriend than her free-spirited self. Every time I talked to Leah, Princess would suddenly appear. When

I played with Leah or tickled her, Princess would start whining and get up under me. A couple of times, she tried to nudge the baby with her nose, which wasn't allowed. Your dog needs to realize that not only does your new baby outrank him in the pecking order, but also this new human is not, in any way, shape, or form, a play toy! (Let me especially caution you against welcoming a new puppy into your home with your baby. If you've ever had a puppy or kitten, you'll remember how high maintenance they can be and how puppies love to bite and nibble on things. And you don't want them biting baby's toes!)

Princess was nine dog years old and fairly well trained when our firstborn arrived. When Lainey was born, Princess was well into her senior years and less willing to change her old ways for a new member in the family, particularly one who screamed all the time.

So, what exactly can we do to help prepare our pets for baby's arrival—in particular, the arrival of a colicky baby? The Humane Society of the United States (www.humanesociety.org) recommends several useful tips to prepare your dog or cat for a new baby, including the following, and reprinted with permission here:

- Take your pet to the veterinarian for a routine health exam and necessary vaccinations.
- Spay or neuter your pet. Not only do sterilized pets typically have fewer health problems associated with their reproductive systems, but they are also calmer and less likely to bite.
- Consult with a veterinarian and pediatrician if the thought of your newborn interacting with the fam-

ily pet makes you uncomfortable.

- Address any pet training and behavior problems. If your pet exhibits fear and anxiety, now is the time to get help from an animal behavior specialist.
- Train your pet to remain calmly on the floor beside you until you invite him on your lap, which will soon cradle a newborn.
- Consider enrolling in a training class with your dog, and practice training techniques. Training allows you to safely and humanely control your dog's behavior and enhances the bond between you and your pet.
- Encourage friends with infants to visit your home to accustom your pet to babies. Supervise all pet and infant interactions.
- Accustom your pet to baby-related noises months before the baby is expected. For example, play recordings of a baby crying, turn on the mechanical infant swing, and use the rocking chair. Make these positive experiences for your pet by offering a treat or playtime.
- To discourage your pet from jumping on the baby's crib and changing table, apply double-stick tape to the furniture.
- If the baby's room will be off-limits to your pet, install a sturdy barrier such as a removable gate (available at pet or baby supply stores) or, for jumpers, even a screen door. Because these barriers still allow your pet to see and hear what's happening in the room, he'll feel less isolated from the family and more comfortable with the new baby noises.

- Use a baby doll to help your pet get used to the real thing. Carry around a swaddled baby doll, take the doll in the stroller when you walk your dog, and use the doll to get your pet used to routine baby activities, such as bathing and diaper changing.
- Talk to your pet about the baby, using the baby's name if you've selected one.
- Sprinkle baby powder or baby oil on your skin so your pet becomes familiar with the new smells.
- Finally, plan ahead to make sure your pet gets proper care while you're at the birthing center.

There are also things you can do upon baby's arrival to ensure a smooth introduction:

- Make sure you greet your pet upon your first entrance with baby. You can have daddy carry the baby to free up your hands for your pet.
- Reward your pet for good behavior around baby.
- Never leave your new baby and pet unattended together despite how child-friendly you perceive your animal to be.

There is a lot of information available regarding the practical aspects of adding a baby to a dog household, but no one ever bothered to mention some important, yet unsettling truths:

- Whenever you sit down to nurse, your dog will bark
- When you sneak in very quietly to lay the baby down to sleep, your dog will bark
- Deaf dogs bark louder than hearing dogs

- Some animals will urinate on the floor to remind the baby whose territory they are in
- Pushing a stroller and walking a dog at the same time can be a very challenging experience
- Some babies are horrified of animals
- Dog hair is like a heat-seeking missile—it seems to always end up on your sweet little baby

You most likely love your pet too much to give her away, and this will drive you mad. But it is in your pet's, and family's, best interest if you can make it through these rough few months. Unless, of course, your animal has ever attempted to harm your baby.

When it comes down to it, a dog is a woman's best friend. They are 100 percent loyal, always happy to see you, and could care less if you look like hell worn over. Their hair and bad manners, however, will undoubtedly drive you completely batty during the colic months. But rest assured you will both get through it. Just keep your pet fed, hydrated, and loved. As for the five-walks-a-day routine and weekly trips to the doggy park, these may have to be put on temporary hold—unless a good walk in the park, where nobody cares if your infant hollers, is just the refresher you need. Don't worry, though. Your pup will be fine and, in his doggy-like fashion, will undoubtedly completely forgive you for these temporary inconveniences.

24

The Other Mommies

LURKING AROUND CORNERS AND DOWN EVERY STORE AISLE IS a person brimming with advice. Big, small, young, and old, there are strangers who will approach you with their colic-soothing strategies with every step you take. Knowing when to run and when to listen will help ease the stress of these unavoidable confrontations.

First, let me say that strangers are called strangers for a reason. We don't know who they are, where they came from, where they are going, or why they are going there. It would be wonderful if we lived in *Leave It to Beaver* land and could stop to offer lifts to every Tom, Dick, and Harry walking down the side of the road. If you did that today you would most surely end up floating in a river somewhere. I would love it if every time a person approached me to collect money for their dying relative that they were, in fact, telling the truth.

My husband calls me mean for not stopping to help strangers, but I consider myself damn smart for not doing so. I'll never forget the time my girls and I were heading to the video store to pick out the newest release when suddenly an older woman came running toward our van. We had just stopped at a stop sign as this stranger approached us, waving her arms about, trying to get me to roll down the window and talk to her. Of course, I did nothing of the sort. I kept right on moving and for good reason: I wanted us all to live. The parking lot was filled with cars and all of the two dozen-plus stores were open, and I am sure inside each and every one were those gadgets we call phones! So why was she flagging down my dusty minivan? I really didn't want to know. Sorry.

Now, if this woman had been bleeding or had a piece of glass sticking out of her head, surely I would have been more receptive to her pleas. Approach me in a public place for help, and I am all ears. Corner me in a dark alley with my kids in tow, and I am high-tailing it out of there.

More often than not, though, your run-ins will be with people who want to give out advice rather than take what is yours. And a screaming baby seems to be a welcomed invitation for all sorts of strangers. In general, there are three distinct categories of advice-givers, and all are females:

1. Super Moms
2. Compassionate Moms
3. Grand Moms

THE SUPER MOM

Knowing what to do depends on whom you are dealing with. Let me start with the most difficult and nail biting of them all: The dreaded super mom. This is the woman who is convinced that she holds her doctorate in mothering. She has been there, done that, and knows it all. She is the type who claims she never had to offer her baby a pacifier to "plug him up" and never had problems getting her baby to sleep. Oh no, her babies were quiet, content, and all figments of her imagination! But she will come to you when you are in your most vulnerable state. She will wait for your baby to start screaming, and watch as you pick her up, pat her back, and even whip out your boob to try to feed her. After she witnesses you fail with every soothing maneuver, she will slowly approach. Holding her head high, and wearing that annoying little smirk, she will confidently prance her way toward you and your screeching infant. Of course, this is easy for her to do since she is kid-free at the moment. All of her kids survived the colic months and terrible two's and are now in school, and this is why she is smiling, sparkling, and dressed in an outfit that matches.

So, what do you do? You can't run, not at least until you put your boob back in. This is when you have to abide by the saying, "Grin and bear it." Bite that tongue, and smile. Gently nod your head and, if possible, come up with a quick excuse to get the hell out of Dodge. Here are some of my favorites:

Excuse #1: "Hi, thanks for the words of wisdom, but we're running late for my pole-dancing class."

Excuse #2: "Thanks. I really need to get going, though. I am dying for a cigarette!"

Excuse #3: "Oh, thanks, I will tell her mom later. I am just the sitter."

These excuses will undoubtedly provide you with a means of escaping the clutches of Misses Know-It-All. It is so hard to not say what is really on your mind, but it's just not worth the wasted air. So, kill her with kindness and deceit!

THE COMPASSIONATE MOM

Now moving on to the compassionate moms. These mothers feel your pain and really want to help you. They do not pass judgment but offer only kind words of encouragement and understanding. Luckily for you, most moms fall into this category. So how can you distinguish between the good and the evil? Super moms usually start a conversation with remarks like, "Your baby really looks like she needs some help," or "Perhaps your baby is cold. I know I am."

Yes, these women are cold and callous and never ask how you, the mother, are coping. On the opposite end of the spectrum are the moms who genuinely want to help you and your baby. They feel your frustrations and usually offer comments regarding your well-being and happiness such as, "Oh, I feel your pain. My baby did the same thing, and I always felt like a total idiot. Don't worry honey, you will get through it." These are the moms you want as your friends, as your neighbors, and as your confidants. It is with these same women you can hold a long conversation about the trials and tribulations of motherhood in the mall food court. She will not care that your baby is screaming but will offer to hold her while you take a bite of your chicken sandwich. She will offer a hug and shoulder to cry on when you need one. And she will remind you that you are human, and if you're lucky will share some tips that she learned along the way. Mothers are our best source of information and inspiration. So, when you meet one of these kind, loving moms, welcome her, and let her help you. You need it and should seize the opportunity.

THE GRAND MOM

On to the last type—the grandmothers. There are a couple different types. Mostly, they are sweet, well-intentioned women with some wise words. Other times, these ladies are way out in left field with parenting advice dating back to BC. For instance, my friend told me her mother brought a parenting book out of the attic that said it was actually good for pregnant women to smoke because it helped decrease their stress. Yeah, that and their baby's oxygen supply. So, what is the best way to deal with grandmotherly advice? Well, I would put the wise ones in the compassionate mom category and treat them as such. As for the ones who offer a swig of whiskey as a cure for colic, you may want to think of some quick, yet kind escape. Just say you really need to get home to get dinner going, or you have to hurry because you think the baby is hungry and every second counts! They will understand.

So, let's pretend, for a moment that you are at my favorite place, the grocery store, checking out and your baby starts screaming. The lady in line behind you says, "Oh goodness. She reminds me of my baby at that age. How are you coping?"

Do you:

1. Respond with a comment fit for a super mom
2. Feel that this lady really gets it, and your response would be the same for a compassionate mom
3. Run

If you answered B, then you are correct! See, it's easy.

I hope you will meet many wonderful, compassionate moms in your community—moms you can share with, bond with, and exchange horror stories with. If an evil super mom ever corners you, just hold your tongue, and remember your experience so that you can share your encounters with these beasts when your children become parents.

Take home this message: Savor moments with the good strangers, run away from the bad ones, and always respect your elders. You can't go wrong with that.

SECTION FIVE
In Case of Emergency
Where to Turn When You're on the Edge

Unlike the other chapters in this book, the following two take on a more serious tone. That is because the main reason I decided to write this book was to save lives—including the mother's and the baby's. Chapter 25 discusses the importance of walking away when you have reached your limit and reveals the importance of never, ever shaking a baby. Shaken baby syndrome kills, and it is avoidable. In Chapter 26, I share my own struggle with postpartum depression. You'll hear how, despite my depression, I made it out of colic physically unscathed. Mentally, I will never be the same, and that's a good thing; I learned a lot along the way. I hope that the following chapters will help answer some important questions, encourage you to get help if you need it, and provide you with the reassurance that you need during this difficult time in your life.

25

Walk—or Run—to the Next Room

BEFORE I HAD LAINEY, I NEVER UNDERSTOOD HOW A PERSON could harm an innocent baby, especially their very own. After my colic experience, I was still sickened by these unsettling news events but could unfortunately understand them a bit better. You see, no one ever told me that I had a one-in-five chance of having a baby that would not stop crying. And no one ever prepared me for how upsetting this would be. So when I started to have ill thoughts toward my baby, I was sure I was the worst mother in the world.

When Lainey was born, she slept in a bassinet that I kept pulled up next to my bed so that I could be close to her, checking to see that her little chest was moving up and down whenever she slept. I even went so far as to put a movement monitor under the bassinet pad that would set off an alarm should she ever stop breathing. After she turned colicky on me, though, I began pushing her bassinet farther and farther away from my bed and no longer compulsively checked to see whether or not she was breathing every time she napped. I know it may not sound that bad to you, but to my obsessive-compulsive self, my failure to check up on my baby was horrendous! This was only the beginning.

It was when Lainey was about six weeks old that I started to care less whether or not I was dead or alive. And as I would hold Lainey in my arms at night trying to console her, trying to get her to sleep, I envisioned myself holding her up and shouting, "What the hell is wrong with you? Why won't you stop crying? Can't you see you're driving me crazy?" Actually, I think I did mention these thoughts to her in passing, not that she knew what I was saying at the time. I took her cries so personally, like an attack on my mothering skills. Didn't she know how much I loved her? If she did, why did she act like she hated me all of the time?

Ever since I was a little girl, all I ever wanted was to be a mother. And when I graduated from pharmacy school, I was seven months pregnant with my first child, second pregnancy. I had miscarried my first baby, right around the time of 9/11. My baby was needed up in heaven to comfort all the souls that ascended on that dreadful day. When I first saw blood, I felt in my heart that something was wrong. That was one of the most depressing events of my life. Losing a child, no matter how young it is, is the worst pain a mother can ever experience.

It was therefore with great glee that I announced the birth of both of my girls. I was overcome with joy and thankfulness with each of their births. So when my perfect little baby turned into a gassy little fuss bucket, I was completely floored.

I honestly believe it is the good moms who have such

a hard time with their difficult-to-soothe babies. Bad moms don't give a damn whether their baby cries or not. But the good ones do—and they're the ones who are hit the hardest. From the moment of conception, these moms do everything they are told. They eat the right foods, take their vitamins, and avoid cigarettes and alcohol. They do their best at breast-feeding, and many are fortunate enough to have success at it. (As a side note, there are millions of wonderful mothers out there who choose not to breast-feed, for whatever reason, and that is fine too. It is purely a mother's choice.) These same good moms let their nesting instinct take over and work hard at making sure their house is just right for their new baby's grand entrance. Then, two weeks after the baby arrives, she begins to cry. And she cries and cries, for no apparent reason. Nothing consoles her, not even your boob. This is when the vicious ride ensues, and you begin circling the hamster wheel of ineptness, inadequacy, insecurity, and instability.

Luckily, I was stable enough, I guess, and never ended up hurting my baby, or myself for that matter, but I did think about it. It wasn't until I dove into some good, from-the-heart discussions with other moms that I realized my ill feelings toward my baby were quite common. Admitting to others that there was even a fraction of a second that I disliked my child is a hard thing to do. Although I never once lost my love for Lainey, I really didn't want to be around her that much when she was screaming her lungs out. Confessing your imperfections to fellow moms is kind of like coming out of the closet. It's hard to do, but once you come out, you feel better.

Besides admitting I wasn't perfect, I also discovered

some other truths that might be of help during this rough time:

Truth #1: A baby will not break from crying but will break if shaken.

Truth#2: Your baby will not remember the colicky days, but you will remember every second.

Truth #3: When you reach your breaking point, put the baby in a safe place, and learn to just walk away.

Truth #4: According to a study published in a respected health journal, approximately 70 percent of mothers had aggressive thoughts and fantasies toward their colicky infants. Twenty-six percent admitted to thoughts of killing their baby. Some moms fantasized about smothering their baby with a pillow, and others dreamt of throwing their baby out the window. These were ordinary women and all were married. I imagine these numbers would be higher among women with no support system living in not-so-favorable conditions. These findings sound horrible, I know, but they are real. It is actually "normal" to have these ill thoughts but it is never normal to act on them.

If you ever have the urge to shake your baby, call 911. Inconsolable crying, as seen in colicky infants, is the number-one trigger for shaken baby syndrome (SBS) and the results are often deadly. Shaking a baby or young child for a mere five seconds can cause brain damage and death. Those who survive SBS can suffer from permanent damage including paralysis, blindness, and profound mental retardation.

Between twelve hundred to fourteen hundred babies in America suffer from SBS each year, and approximately

one-third of these babies will die as a result. It is important for you to learn to recognize the symptoms of SBS,
especially if you have to return to work or have someone
else watch your baby during the fussy months. Make sure
you emphasize, and re-emphasize, to your child's caregiver
that they can call you when they are at their wits' end. Let
them know that you will be there in a flash if they need
assistance and that it is never an inconvenience for them
to call for help—it is a necessity. You know how hard it
is for you to keep your cool. Others might not have all that
love inside to prevent them from doing the unthinkable:
shaking a baby.

Here are some of the warning signs of SBS:

- unequal-sized pupils and/or difficulty focusing on
  objects
- change in eating habits: poor sucking and/or swal-
  lowing
- unexplained vomiting
- tremors
- unusual tiredness or limpness
- no smiling or facial expressions
- failure to thrive
- irritability
- pale or bluish skin
- seizures

If you ever think that someone has shaken your baby,
or if you notice any of the warning signs listed above, seek
immediate medical attention for your baby, and alert social services and law enforcement authorities. It is imperative to never let anyone watch your baby if you think for

one second that they may hurt your child. There is always someone you can call for help, and Appendix II lists many of these toll-free numbers for you. All you have to do is pick up the phone.

Remember, you are not a Stepford wife—you are a real, live human being. You were born with the beautiful imperfections of womankind, and you have many feelings to contend with. Next time your baby starts into one of her inconsolable fits, do the normal routine of changing, feeding, burping, cuddling, and so forth, and then put her down in a safe place and let her "sing," as some call it. It's okay to let her cry it out for five or ten minutes. The hardest part is letting go of the guilt and allowing yourself to close the door, walk away, and regain your composure. Rest assured, there are plenty of other mothers going through the same thing right now. Try to find them so that you can help each other out.

After you walk away, it's best to engage in something that will help calm your nerves such as the following:

- Go outside and listen to the birds sing
- Call a friend and vent
- Vacuum (the noise muffles the cries!)
- Recite your colic mantra:
  May I possess the inner strength of Hercules
  May I harbor the patience of Job
  May I take no cries personally
  May I throw away all guilt
  May my baby and I love each other for eternity
  Om peace, peace, peace.

26

Reach Out and Grab Someone

"You can turn painful situations around through laughter. If you can find humor in anything—even poverty—you can survive it." —Bill Cosby

AS YOU MAY HAVE ALREADY GATHERED, I AM SLIGHTLY PARA-noid when it comes to the welfare of my family. The first thing I do, after safely strapping both girls in their car seats and adjusting the side and rear view mirrors, is to make sure I remember to lock all the doors. Who would want to take the risk of some stranger popping into your vehicle at a stop sign and directing you to the closest bank? My husband would always kid me about my obsession with locking everything up, but I was, and still am, a very cautious individual.

When I stopped locking up my van like Fort Knox, I knew something wasn't quite right. In fact, I did quite the opposite when I was alone. Instead of keeping the windows up high enough so no one could reach in, I rolled them all the way down. My doors were unlocked, and I could have cared less if someone wanted to carjack me. If I were dead, I would at least be free, I thought.

It was after the thoughts of suicide danced in my head

that I knew I was in real trouble. I imagined myself clearing out all of the junk in the garage to make enough room for my minivan. Then, I could see myself closing the garage door, climbing into the van, turning on the ignition, and peacefully drifting off. But luckily at that point I was still well enough to realize that my death would be detrimental to my girls, and to my husband. I envisioned my girls at my funeral, sobbing violently with their daddy by their side. I never ever wanted my girls to feel that kind of pain, so I knew that somehow, some way, I had to get better.

I also knew that I could not beat this thing alone. Instead, I had to conjure up enough strength to open myself up to my husband and reveal my dark fantasies and thoughts of suicide. I wanted to ensure that, in my deepest states of depression, I never actually tried to kill myself. Yes, I was very ill, but I realized that, in the end, I wanted to make it through the colic months alive. The evenings of torture, the pacing back and forth for hours each day to get Lainey to quiet down, and the struggle to care for two girls with my husband working day and night were ruthless. But I knew that things would eventually get better. I just needed to muster up enough strength to make it through the next few months so that one day I could witness the birth of my own grandchildren. After my husband discovered how needy I was, he grabbed me by the hand and directed me to a medical professional.

My diagnosis was postpartum depression (PPD). I had always associated depression with crying all the time for no reason, but I was actually suffering more from aggression and irritability. I would snap at Leah for no reason

and had two-year-old temper tantrums. But after read-
ing up on PPD, I came to realize that some mothers do
experience more madness than sadness. And having a
high-needs baby most likely contributed to the severity
of it.

Approximately 15 percent of all new mothers experience postpartum depression, and it often goes undiag-
nosed and untreated. This is a shame, especially since it
is 100 percent treatable. It's so important to know you are
not alone and to learn how to recognize the symptoms of
a true depression, as well as symptoms of a transient
case of the "baby blues." So, I turned to Dr. Shoshana Bennett, Ph.D., author of *Postpartum Depression for Dummies*,
to help shed some light on the differences between these
postpartum issues, and I quote below from her book,
with permission:

*After giving birth, it's perfectly normal for a woman
to have a bout of what has been affectionately labeled
"the baby blues." Research shows that between 50 and
85 percent of all new moms experience the baby blues.
The blues can persist for two or possibly even three
weeks but for the most part they dissipate by the end
of the second week. Feelings often include one or more
of the following:*

- *Weepiness*
- *Stress*
- *Vulnerability*
- *Sadness*
- *Worry*
- *Lack of concentration*

I think these symptoms can be found in almost every new mom out there! Luckily, however, these feelings are very common and do not require the help of a professional.

POSTPARTUM DEPRESSION

PPD and the baby blues look similar in some ways: They both involve some kind of low mood, worry, and feelings of sadness and irritability, and they both affect new moms. But PPD is a more serious condition that requires a completely different level of intervention than the baby blues. Because of the seriousness of PPD, you need to know how to tell the difference between the two so you can get help as soon as possible.

Here are two ways to differentiate the baby blues for PPD:

Duration of symptoms: *The first way to tell the difference is by noting how long your symptoms last— regardless of how mild they may seem. Anything past two (or at the most, three) weeks, even if you feel only mildly blue, is now considered PPD.*

Severity of symptoms: *If, as a new mom, your symptoms interfere with your daily life in a big way, you may be suffering from PPD or another postpartum disorder. If your symptoms are in fact strong enough to affect your daily life, you need to contact a professional, even if it happens to overlap the baby blues timing of the first two weeks (or so) after pregnancy. The sooner you get help, the better.*

The following list comprises just some of the most common feelings, symptoms, and emotions related to PPD:

- *Sleeping too much or inability to sleep at night, even when you're not up with your baby*
- *Irritability, hostility, or rage*
- *Worrying much of the time*
- *Feeling overwhelmed or anxious*
- *Difficulty making even minor decisions*
- *Problems concentrating and lack of focus*
- *Change in appetite (usually loss of, but sometimes the opposite)*
- *Overeating or binging on carbs and sugar*
- *Loss of sex drive*
- *Sad a majority of the time*
- *Guilty feelings*
- *Low self-esteem or feelings of worthlessness*
- *Hopelessness*
- *Inability to experience pleasure*
- *Discomfort with the baby (uncomfortable holding or interacting with the baby)*
- *Physical problems without apparent cause (backaches or other pains that the doctor can't figure out)*

Thoughts of suicide are another very important symptom of PPD that require immediate help. And it is best to treat PPD as early on as possible to help minimize any effects it may have on that wonderful bond formed between mother and baby. The best person to turn to is a licensed psychologist who specializes in postpartum issues. You can also ask your obstetrician, primary care doctor, or even your baby's pediatrician for proper referrals to ensure you receive the care and attention you deserve.

Through my experiences lecturing on the topic of coping with colic, I've discovered that many cultures do not believe in treating depression. Mothers are often ashamed for feeling ill thoughts toward their baby and themselves and are discouraged by their friends and relatives to seek professional help. They don't want anyone to think they are "crazy." Well, we know these women are not crazy. They are suffering from a real chemical imbalance and need help. No one should be ashamed to acknowledge that they are feeling depressed and, most important, you owe it to your children to make sure that you are at your best and able to properly care for them. So, if you are one of the women out there whose family and friends are ignoring your pleas for help, go seek it on your own. You don't have to tell them about it. Just go do it for your own and your baby's sake.

I believe I had an unfair advantage over many women suffering from PPD due to my medical background and pharmacy experience. Most women have no idea that a good percentage of our population is on antidepressants. Doctor, lawyers, teachers, butchers, bakers, and candlestick makers—many of them are on Prozac, Lexapro, or Paxil. All three of these drugs can be used to treat PPD and other types of mood disorders. I knew that I would not be labeled as some crazy loon because I had to take Lexapro, for goodness sake. It's one of the most popular drugs dispensed by our nation's pharmacies! And antidepressant drugs, combined with counseling, can really help women suffering from PPD. These drugs help restore that delicate balance that has shifted at our child's birth and, most important, they can help save lives.

Most of us have heard of the horrible tragedy surrounding Andrea Yates, the woman who drowned her five young children in the bathtub. She suffered from a very serious condition known as postpartum psychosis (PPP). This disorder usually presents itself within the first or second week postpartum and is a completely different animal than PPD. Considered a rare disorder, PPP affects only one or two in one thousand women postpartum, but when you look at the average number of children born each year in the United States, this equates to approximately eight thousand PPP sufferers. And, these women have a 5 percent suicide rate and a 4 percent infanticide rate. The most concerning aspect of PPP is that the mother often has no idea that anything is wrong with her. According to Dr. Bennett, the main reactions associated with postpartum psychosis are:

- *Auditory hallucinations (hearing things others don't, such as "special messages" meant only for her from the TV, radio, computer, or newspaper)*
- *Bizarre thoughts about needing to kill her baby*
- *Confusion*
- *Disorientation*
- *Extreme agitation*
- *Insomnia*
- *Paranoia (false beliefs that others are trying to harm her)*
- *Tactile hallucinations (feeling things that aren't there, for instance spiders crawling up her arm)*
- *Visual hallucinations (seeing things others don't)*

It's usually a relative or friend who first notices symptoms of postpartum psychosis (PPP). These women may swear up and down that their life is normal, yet at the same time they will be sewing purple daisies onto their husband's dress suits. And it is important to be aware of some of the risk factors that have been linked to the development of PPP, including a personal or family history of psychosis or bipolar disorder. Also, if a mother has had PPP before, then she has a 70 percent chance of suffering from it again. It is therefore imperative that these women receive the proper medical care they need immediately. If not, the results can be deadly.

Most of you will not suffer from PPD and even fewer will suffer from PPP. But having a very high-needs baby can increase your chances of falling into a depressed state. Luckily for you and your family, there are many professionals and a lot of information available dedicated to helping women transform from tired, hopeless moms into spunky, joyful nurturers. There are hotlines, Web sites, support groups, and books—all devoted to helping you get through these tough times. Please refer to Appendix II for some appropriate references on this topic.

Colicky infants can bring out the worst in you. But they will make you stronger. With every twist and turn, you will gain strength, momentum, and the confidence to keep moving forward. Overcoming postpartum depression was not an easy task for me, but I had no other choice. I wanted to live, and here I am, alive and kicking!

27

You're Almost There!

"Your success and happiness lie in you. Resolve to keep happy, and your joy and you shall form an invisible host against difficulties." —Helen Keller

IT IS AMAZING HOW PERFECTLY THE EVENTS OF OUR LIVES tend to fall into place. Although you would never know it while they are happening, the obstacles we face always have reason and purpose behind them. Take me, for instance. Never in a million years did I think I would become the person I am today. A mother of two, a pharmacist, a lover of chocolate, and an author.

Once I became a mother, my confidence grew a thousand-fold. The mere fact that my body was capable of producing another human being, and carrying that same person for ten months, made me feel that I could do just about anything. Thank God for that confidence booster because, if it were not for my first daughter turning out so well, I don't know that I could have survived the colicky months with my second daughter at all. But when Lainey was born, I knew that everything I was doing was the right thing to do, most of the time. And if Lainey had been my firstborn, she would have been my last. Not because she didn't turn out perfectly in the end, but because colic is so hard on your self-esteem and sense of competence that I would have doubted my abilities to handle the same situation ever again.

Just think about all of the challenges life has handed you and how many of them framed the foundation for where you are today. Were you forced to grow up too quickly? Did you have a mother or father who was absent? Have you ever been deeply hurt, either mentally or physically? Did you have to date a lot of jerks before you finally met the man of your dreams? And, most important, do you know what your dreams are?

I discovered that my difficult high school years were, in fact, full of purpose. It was my desire to show all of my classmates up one day that drove me to become successful. I learned that having a guidance counselor who was a little rough around the edges was just what I needed, at the time, to get me going. Because my relationship between my parents was not exactly the best, I knew that I needed to pick a profession that enabled me to support myself and my family on my own, if need be. And after going to hell and back with a colicky infant, I learned how important it was to see the humor in life, and that, no matter how bad you think you've got it, everything does happen for a reason. You just have to figure out what that reason is, and make the best of it.

Before I even thought about writing this book, I came up with the idea of CRI, which stands for the Colic Relief Initiative. This initiative would allow the formation of community CRI centers where parents could go, with crying baby in hand, and seek support. These centers would allow moms and dads to escape for an hour or two, so that they could regain their strength and composure. If you have the will and the way to start one of these centers, do it. It will help save lives.

Try to channel all of your negative energy into something positive in the end. Write about your experiences, share your stories with other moms, and enter online parenting forums to encourage other mothers living with colic. It helps so much to hear loving and hopeful words from fellow moms who have been there and done that. Hold their hands, give them hugs, and show them your support.

My girls have taught me more than I ever imagined—how to love, forgive, and laugh, even when I don't feel like laughing. I am still discovering life's lessons every day. With each sunrise and each sunset I am handed a new set of challenges. And while knowing you are not in total control of your life may be a difficult concept to grasp, it will help you breathe easier. So sit back, try your best, and let things fall into place as they will.

If you met Lainey now, you would never, for one second, believe that she had been colicky. She is now the most fun, outgoing two-year-old girl you could meet. Colic left our household when she was about eleven weeks old, and my life with her has been on the up and up ever since. Now, instead of screaming when people approach her, she blows them kisses. She is that sweet little girl you've seen in the store who says "Hi" and waves to absolutely every single man, woman, and child who walks by. Everyone who meets Lainey loves her, and she loves them equally. Her smiles are genuine, her giggles are heartwarming, and her skin is still soft to the touch. She is teetering in between that baby and little girl stage, and

I am holding onto every baby moment she has left.

No one will ever understand the hell that surrounds living with a colicky baby unless they have experienced it for themselves. Once you have survived it, you will be changed forever. I hope that you have learned from my mistakes, laughed at my imperfections, and discovered how terrific it feels to survive such an enormous challenge. I know you didn't ask for your baby to have colic, it just happened. And as with other bends in the road of life, you learn to adjust. Just remember, in the game of life you are never dealt cards that you can't trump.

May God bless you and your family.

APPENDICES

Appendix I
The Colic Commandments

- Thou shall not steal, unless you're stealing a handful of babysitters.

- Thou shall not run away and join the circus.

- Thou shall run away and get a massage.

- Thou shall not attempt to see through the dust encapsulating the dining room table.

- Thou shall buy frozen dinners and paper plates.

- Thou shall always accept help when offered.

- Thou shall not feel guilty for purchasing your fifth remote control. (Somehow they keep flying out the window . . .)

- Thou shall not ever harm your baby or yourself.

- Thou shall listen to Jimmy Buffett for some changes in attitude, especially when on the verge of a breakdown.

- Thou shall laugh at least once, very loudly, every day.

Appendix II
Important Resources

PHONE NUMBERS
National Child Abuse Hotlines
National Center on Shaken Baby Syndrome Hotline:
    (888) 273-0071
Childhelp® USA National Child Abuse Hotline:
    (800) 4ACHILD (800-422-4453)

Regional Child Abuse Numbers
Alabama (AL), (334) 242-9500
Alaska (AK), (800) 478-4444
Arizona (AZ), (888) SOS-CHILD (888-767-2445)
Arkansas (AR), (800) 482-5964
California (CA), (916) 445-2832
Colorado (CO), (303) 866-5932
Connecticut (CT), (800) 842-2288, (800) 624-5518
    (TDD/Hearing Impaired)
Delaware (DE), (800) 292-9582
District of Columbia (DC), (202) 671-7233
Florida (FL), (800) 96-ABUSE (800-962-2873)
Georgia (GA), (404) 657-7660
Hawaii (HI), (808) 832-5300
Idaho (ID), (800) 600-6474

Illinois (IL), (800) 252-2873
Indiana (IN), (800) 800-5556
Iowa (IA), (800) 362-2178
Kansas (KS), (800) 922-5330
Kentucky (KY), (800) 752-6200
Louisiana (LA), (225) 925-4571
Maine (ME), (800) 452-1999
Maryland (MD), (800) 332-6347
Massachusetts (MA), (800) 792-5200
Michigan (MI), (800) 942-4357
Minnesota (MN), (651) 296-8337
Mississippi (MS), (800) 222-8000
Missouri (MO), (800) 392-3738
Montana (MT), (800) 332-6100
Nebraska (NE), (800) 652-1999
Nevada (NV), (800) 992-5757
New Hampshire (NH), (800) 894-5533
New Jersey (NJ), (800) 792-8610, (800) 835-5510
    (TDD/Hearing Impaired)
New Mexico (NM), (800) 797-3260
New York (NY), (800) 342-3720
North Carolina (NC), (800) 662-7030
North Dakota (ND), (800) 245-3736
Oklahoma (OK), (800) 522-3511
Ohio (OH), (614) 466-9274
Oregon (OR), (800) 854-3508
Pennsylvania (PA), (800) 932-0313
Rhode Island (RI), (800) RI-CHILD (800-742-4453)
South Carolina (SC), (803) 734-0220
South Dakota (SD), (800) 227-3020
Tennessee (TN), (615) 742-9192

Texas (TX), (800) 252-5400
Utah (UT), (800) 678-9399
Vermont (VT), (800) 649-5285
Virginia (VA), (800) 552-7096
Washington (WA), (800) 562-5624
West Virginia (WV), (800) 352-6513
Wyoming (WY), (800) 457-3659

Postpartum Depression Hotlines
Postpartum Stress Line, (888) 678-2669
Postpartum Support International, (800) 944-4773
National Hopeline Network, (800) 773-6667

WEB SITES
Child Abuse Prevention
National Center on Shaken Baby Syndrome,
    www.dontshake.org
The SKIPPER Initiative, www.skippervigil.com
Prevent Child Abuse America, www.preventchildabuse.org

Postpartum Depression
Postpartum Assistance for Mothers,
    www.postpartumdepressionhelp.com
The Online PPD Support Group, www.ppdsupport.com
Postpartum Dads, www.postpartumdads.org

Support/Parenting Groups
The Mommies Network,
    www.themommiesnetwork.org
International MOMS Club, www.momsclub.org
MOPS International, www.mops.org

For Laughs

Sanity Central, www.sanitycentral.com (a laughter time-out from parenting)

Comedy Cures, www.comedycures.org (a nonprofit organization dedicated to providing kids and adults with therapeutic humor programs)

Jackie Papandrew's Web site, www.jackiepapandrew.com ("Airing My Dirty Laundry" is Papandrew's hilarious column about parenting and life)

W. Bruce Cameron's Web site, www.wbrucecameron.com (a nationally syndicated humor columnist)

Where I Live, www.timbete.com (another funny dad and columnist)

Appendix III
Recommended Reading

Postpartum Depression for Dummies, by Dr. Shoshana
   Bennett, Ph.D. (Hoboken, NJ: Wiley Publishing,
   2007).

*Beyond the Blues: A Guide to Understanding and Treating
   Prenatal and Postpartum Depression,* by Dr. Shoshana
   Bennett, Ph.D., and Pec Indman (San Jose, CA:
   Moodswings Press, 2006).

Baby Massage: Soothing Strokes for Healthy Growth, by
   Suzanne Reese (New York: Viking Studio, 2006).

Your Pregnancy Week by Week, by Glade B. Curtis, M.D.,
   M.P.H., and Judith Schuler, M.S., sixth ed. (New York:
   Da Capo Lifelong, 2008)

Babywearing, by Dr. Maria Blois (Amarillo, TX:
   Pharmasoft Publishing, 2005).

Appendix IV
The Colic Countdown Calendar

How to use this calendar:

1. For every day of colic you survive, mark a big X on your calendar. Make sure you do this each and every night before bedtime (or attempt to). For every X, know that you'll earn a reward when your colic days are over.

2. Every other Wednesday is the day you should try to line up babysitters for the following weekend. Most sitters like at least one-week's notice. If you're a real

Week	Sunday	Monday	Tuesday
1: The calm before the storm	Sleep all you can while your help is here		
2: What happened to my sweet baby?	Call back the troops!		
3:	You're probably ready for some earplugs		

planner, then, by all means, go ahead and line up all your date nights in advance at one time. But, in case you forget, the calendar will help remind you. These date nights can be with your husband or older kids who do not cry or throw food on the floors at nice restaurants. Or you can use these nights for some time alone. Just do whatever makes you happy!

3. You need at least two date nights a month. If you're really lucky, you can get one a week! In that case, every Wednesday you should be booking a sitter. When your baby is six weeks old, the colic will probably be at its worst. For this reason, you should try to schedule two date-night weekends in a row, if possible.

4. Colic usually disappears by the time your baby is twelve weeks old. If it lasts longer than that, I am very sorry. But, if this does happen to you, you poor soul, just keep doing what you've been doing and keep planning those nights out.

Wednesday	Thursday	Friday	Saturday
Aren't babies awesome?			Soak in the love
*Schedule date night for next weekend			Take a long relaxing bubble bath
Look forward to your first night out			**Date night**

continued

Week	Sunday	Monday	Tuesday
4	Now is about the time for some head-phones		
5	Invite someone over so you can take a nap (or enlist your husband's help!)		
6: She's Peaking	Think happy thoughts		
7: Where's the off switch?	Take deep breaths and remember to take time-outs		
8	You deserve a medal— and some chocolate!		
9	Your baby should start settling down in the next couple weeks		
10	Recite your colic mantra		
11	Pray really hard that the end is coming		
12: My sweet baby returns!	You did it!		

Wednesday	Thursday	Friday	Saturday
*Call and schedule a sitter for next weekend and the one after that			Vent your frustrations either to a friend or on paper
Your baby loves you regardless of her constant cries			**Date night**
Remember date night is coming			**Date night**
*Schedule date night for next weekend			Rent a movie that makes you laugh like crazy
Think of the stories you can tell!			**Date night**
*Schedule date night for next weekend			Read a really good book
I foresee a very relaxing vacation in your near future			**Date night**
*Schedule your celebration night for next weekend			Make some popcorn and watch *Dirty Dancing*
Give yourself a great big pat on the back and get ready for Saturday			**Celebration night!**

Appendix V
The Chocoholic's Caffeine Content Guide

Compare some of your favorite chocolates to other caffeinated products. Enjoy!

CHOCOLATE PRODUCTS

Product	Serving Size	Average Caffeine Content (mg)
Hershey's Chocolate Bar	1.55 oz	9
Hershey's Special Dark Chocolate Bar	1.45 oz	31
Kit Kat	1.5 oz	6
Krackel Chocolate Bar	1.45 oz	7
Skor Toffee Bar	1.4 oz	3
Mr. Goodbar	1.75 oz	7
Hershey's Kisses	9 pieces	9
Hershey's Goodnight Hugs Hot Cocoa Mix	1 envelope	2
Hershey's Chocolate Syrup	2 Tbsp	7

SOURCE: HERSHEY'S COMPANY 2008

BEVERAGES

Product	Serving Size	Average Caffeine Content (mg)
Starbucks Cappuccino, Short	8 oz	75
Starbucks Decaf Coffee of the Week, Short	8 oz	15
Coca-Cola Classic	8 oz	23
Diet Coke	8 oz	31
Nestea Lemon Sweet	8 oz	11
Diet Nestea Citrus Green	8 oz	11
Pepsi	8 oz	25
Diet Pepsi	8 oz	24
Mountain Dew	8 oz	36
Lipton Iced Tea with Lemon	8 oz	20
Lipton Diet Green Tea with Citrus	8 oz	11

SOURCES: STARBUCKS COFFEE 2008, THE COCA-COLA COMPANY 2008, PEPSI 2008

A percentage of proceeds made from the sale of this book will be donated to several organizations dedicated to protecting the health and safety of our children, including The National Center on Shaken Baby Syndrome, Prevent Child Abuse America, and The SKIPPER Initiative.